Saving Democracy: From the Warnings of 2016 to the Urgency of 2025

Updated and expanded for 2025 by Bob Passi

Saving Democracy: From the Warnings of 2016 to the Urgency of 2025

Updated and Expanded Edition

This is a revised and expanded edition of the author's earlier work: Saving Democracy: *The 2016 Presidential Election-The 2016 Presidential Election: An American Watershed,* © 2016 by R.W. Passi.

ISBN: 979-8-9990453-0-0

Library of Congress Control Number: 2025911370

First edition: 2025

Published by Bob Passi

Printed in the United States of America

This is a work of nonfiction. The views expressed are those of the author.

Contact at: bobpassi@charter.net

Website: www.perspectives-bobpassi.org

2

Table of Contents

Saving Democracy-2025

Saving Democracy:
From the Warnings of 2016
To the Urgency of 2025

Preface-May 2025

Introduction

More than nine years ago, in 2016, I published the first version of *Saving Democracy: The 2016 Presidential Election—An American Watershed.* It was written in response to the stunning election of Donald Trump as president and the Republican Party's dramatic resurgence.

That election had seemed destined to go the other way. Hillary Clinton was the presumed favorite. The Republican Party appeared fractured—on the verge of collapse—after a chaotic primary featuring 17 candidates and what felt like an endless stream of clowns emerging from a tiny car.

Yet from that circus emerged Donald Trump, a television personality and political novice with the bombast of a carnival barker. He brought raw spectacle to the campaign trail—less policy than performance. And while seasoned politicians dismissed him as entertainment, the media couldn't look away. He dominated airtime not because he was taken seriously, but because he drove ratings with his outrage and bravado.

While the Democratic National Committee operated on autopilot—courting Wall Street, Big Tech, and corporate donors—it failed to see a deeper shift underway. Working-class Americans, long assumed to be loyal, were beginning to feel not just ignored, but abandoned.

5

These were ordinary citizens—people who provided the labor behind America's prosperity but were seeing fewer rewards. They were politically homeless. In many ways, they echoed the early American colonists: taxed, governed, but unrepresented.

Trump saw a market. He didn't need a platform—he needed a pitch. He offered them visibility, voice, and the promise of disruption. He accepted their frustrations and, for many, their biases. He made them feel seen.

Ironically, the Democrats had another candidate who also spoke to that same neglected constituency: Bernie Sanders. Virtually ignored by the media and without major funding, he built a grassroots movement grounded in New Deal ideals. His message drew enormous crowds, energized young voters, and challenged corporate politics from within.

The contrast between Clinton's high-dollar fundraising events and Sanders' volunteer-driven rallies was stark. The real contest wasn't just between parties—it was between energies: Trump's spectacle and Sanders' grassroots momentum.

Then came the betrayal. The Democratic National Committee undermined Sanders' campaign, ensuring Clinton's nomination. The cost was enormous. Disillusioned Sanders supporters watched their movement dismantled from within. Some were left with only one candidate who acknowledged their existence: Donald Trump.

Trump won. The DNC's bet failed. Clinton had no coattails. Down-ballot Democrats suffered. A newly reconstituted Republican coalition—now fused with a disaffected working class—surged to national dominance. Democrats clung to outdated narratives in a political landscape they no longer recognized.

It was a political earthquake. Years of neglected needs and growing frustration had erupted. The tectonic plates of

6

American politics shifted, shattering old assumptions and revealing a new political terrain.

It was a watershed moment. Yet many in the Democratic establishment continued to act as though nothing had changed—ignoring the shift and clinging to a familiar but outdated map. That denial proved costly.

In this altered terrain, the conventional wisdom no longer applied. The challenge wasn't merely political—it was existential: Could American democracy adapt? Could any party rise to meet this moment?

This *Updated 2025 Edition* of *Saving Democracy* begins by revisiting the forces that led to the 2016 election. But more importantly, it charts what followed: the Trump presidency, the Democratic response, the Biden years, the election of 2024, and the shocking return of Donald Trump to the White House.

It also examines the first 100 days of Trump's second administration and its aggressive assault on democratic institutions—from the rule of law to the Constitution itself. We'll explore the shifting of wealth, the dismantling of government programs, the unraveling of global alliances, and the rise of authoritarianism.

Most crucially, this edition expands on the only remaining source of democratic power: the citizen. Because in the face of institutional decay, it is citizens—not parties—who hold the last line of defense.

Let us begin.

Section I:
The Warnings of 2016

Saving Democracy-The 2016 Presidential Election: An American Earthquake

December 2016

Perspective

> *In earlier times, from the perspective of the earth, the orbits of the planets made no sense, unless strange and arcane explanations were applied. When it was suggested that the perspective be shifted to the sun-centered universe the orbits of the planets became clear and even simple and elegant.*

Introduction

A watershed is, in geological terms, the point where water flow is divided—streams on one side flow in one direction, and those on the other flow the opposite way.

For a nation, a watershed moment is a time when its future direction is about to be decided. That choice can determine the trajectory of a nation for decades, if not longer.

These watershed moments are often triggered by major—and frequently traumatic—events.

This is not the first watershed moment in our history. The first was the traumatic and revolutionary break from England—choosing independence over continued colonial status. The choice was between forming a democracy or continuing under the control of a monarchy and its economic aristocracy, both of which profited from America as a colony. The conflict was democracy versus domination by a foreign economic elite—though some in America merely sought to replace the English aristocracy with an American version.

The second national trauma was the American Civil War, which pitted a Southern economic aristocracy built on the plantation system and slavery against the Northern ideal of free labor and a more democratic, humane treatment of citizens—though both visions were deeply flawed in execution.

The third national trauma was the stock market crash of 1929, plunging the nation—and the world—into a long depression. The crash was largely caused by an unrestrained economic aristocracy, running amok and nearly bringing the entire nation to ruin. In response, FDR initiated sweeping social and economic reforms, moving the nation significantly closer to democracy.

All of these watershed moments stemmed from a fundamental conflict between the direction an economic elite wanted to take the nation and the direction a democratic citizenry would choose.

Time and again, Americans chose democracy over domination by an economic elite.

Now, we face another of those traumatic watershed moments. We will need to choose our future. Will we, as in the past, reclaim democracy—or will we finally surrender to domination by an economic aristocracy?

9

Time for another gut check of the vaunted American Spirit.

In effect, we are occupied. The American Dream we once passionately supported—and for which we even fought and died—has been displaced. In its place stands a system ruled by an economic aristocracy.

The relationship between the people and their leaders has been warped beyond recognition. This has happened while we were distracted by the promises of an alien ideology, now called neoliberal economics. Our democracy—and our relationship with our government—have been transformed into something we barely recognize.

The last election brought us face to face with this new reality, shattering any illusions that the American Dream was still intact.

In its effort to protect itself from the democratizing forces of the people, the economic aristocracy has handed control of the nation to a CEO figurehead, empowered by radical right-wing forces.

It was a rude awakening. A moment of disillusionment.

It's like waking to find your spouse in bed with someone else—and realizing it's been going on for years right under your nose, all while you were being reassured that everything was fine and your future together secure. Do you insist on a divorce—or do you simply learn to live with this new reality?

This is the test.

The United States will either remain a nation capable of change and self-correction—or it will become a fixed, static system hardened into a reactionary, radical capitalism of oligarchs and autocrats, locked in place by an impregnable establishment immune to reform.

We either care enough about the nation and its people to stop the hollowing out of its human, democratic heart—or

Saving Democracy-2025

we're willing to let it be replaced by a cold, inhuman, and manipulative mechanism that values wealth and power over human concerns.

We are at a potential watershed moment: either we move back toward our democratic heritage, or we continue down the path of ever-tightening control by an elite that keeps us distracted, divided, poor, and powerless.

This small book is an exploration of what has happened, how it happened, where we are headed if we don't change course—and what it will take to reverse that trajectory. It also offers some suggestions for how to begin.

This is not intended to be a scholarly tome dissecting every detail. It is a way of thinking about our current situation—blending historical and contextual insights with metaphorical and reflective interludes called Perspectives.

After a brief reflection on the 2016 election, I offer some context: a look at the current global dynamics, forms of governance and economics, and the types of societies they produce—especially in contrast to what a healthy and sustainable human society might look like. This includes a glance at the role of establishments in political processes and a short piece on the power of dominant narratives—narratives that often function like spells.

The next section summarizes the evolution of forces and changes in the U.S., with emphasis on the post–New Deal era—how the promise of the American Dream was gradually and cynically subverted by an alien ideology that now dominates our political and economic life.

That is followed by a look at two possible futures. One continues our current trajectory. The other envisions a return to authentic American democracy and a reconstitution of our national identity.

11

Creating that change will require a journey back to democracy—a plan of action that recognizes the need to work largely outside the toxic, corrupted system. It's not a definitive blueprint, but a starting point: a grassroots strategy grounded in the clear, unifying goal of reestablishing democracy.

It is certainly a plan that could—and perhaps must—succeed. What matters is that we begin and allow the process to evolve in the act of doing. Waiting for a perfect plan often leads to paralysis through politics and inaction.

The heart of it all is to focus on the major goal: reestablishing democracy. Then we can build unity, break the isolation so many citizens feel, and ignite the energy, momentum, and creative power of an empowered democratic citizenry.

Finally, there is an appendix—however incomplete—of practical tools, tactics, and techniques that may help make this transformation real.

We've all read books and articles, and heard speakers tell us what's wrong and what must be done—but the solutions they offer too often rely on working within a system designed to resist real change.

I want to offer some more hopeful ideas for how individuals and groups can operate outside that system—to create space for bold energy and creativity, unencumbered by the constraints of institutions controlled by an economic elite.

I want to help pave the way back to a sustainable democracy.

Perspective: An American Oz

This is a story of a people who were seduced by an illusion that promised an idealized future of prosperity and security for which they only had to give over control of their lives and their resources to a group of economic Wizards. Being good and trusting people, they believed their leaders. It was as old as the story of the Pied Piper.

It happened slowly, almost without them knowing what was happening.

It began with the building of a very attractive road. One day they noticed a construction crew beginning to lay the first paving stones of a new road. They were not told where it was going, but they could see that the paving stones appeared to be yellow brick, almost golden.

As the construction continued, they saw that the contractors paid a great deal of attention to detail. They also constructed hotels and restaurants and other roadside attractions to make any trip on that road quite memorable and enjoyable.

Finally, the road was finished, people were encouraged to try it out, to make the trip along this fabulous road to its destination which was promised to be even more incredible.

People were eager to try it out and it was soon filled with smiling travelers and finally, nearly everyone decided to take the trip.

The trip felt like an adventure. It wound through a lush countryside and eventually passed through a huge field of flowers…poppies. At the end of that day the travelers found themselves tired and dreamy and ready for the magnificent hotel that awaited them.

They awoke the next morning in Oz.

They found themselves living in the American Oz…a walled Emerald City. They found a pair of glasses with green lenses beside their beds and were told that everyone in Oz was required to wear them at all times. They found that with the emerald glasses, they could see that green was the color of success and that the more green you wore showed your level of success in Oz. There were even shades of green. Those who were most successful wore darker green and those with the darkest green were allowed to move freely with people making way for them, even with slight bows of.

The society seemed well organized and happy. They learned that there was a President who was elected and was in charge and that he received direction and advice from the Wizard who lived cloaked in secrecy, and when he spoke directly to the people of Oz, he spoke in an awe-inspiring and authoritative voice.

There were, of course, the necessary flying monkeys of the security state, there only to protect Oz from outside threats, but definitely exerting a chilling effect on any disagreeable actions.

Little did the people know that, while they were mesmerized by the illusions of Oz and by the flash and dazzle accompanying it, that all of the foundations of

14

the American Dream and of their heritage of democracy were being undermined and destroyed. While they were in rapture over the eye candy and games in the new entertainment arena, all the basic rules of life in America were being changed.

They saw occasional cracks in the illusion but were quickly distracted with the talk of a new foreign threat, some potential weather disaster, the latest celebrity scandal, or a new war.

There were bubbles bursting around them, but their leaders continued to tell them to keep the faith and stay the course and that major threats could be withstood with duct-tape, sheets of plastic and continued shopping.

They felt their sense of community dwindling as they were told that everyone was only responsible for themselves. They answered the calls for more austerity but saw that it only led to more prosperity for those on top.

The walls were beginning to develop cracks, and the idea that nothing good existed outside the walls was beginning to be questioned. There were even some who had removed their glasses for a time and reported that what looked green with the glasses was only grey in reality...not only that, but it was looking pretty old and tattered.

Some people remembered what life was like before the yellow brick road and the spell of the poppies. They remembered life in an American Democracy.

15

Some had even seen behind the curtain of secrecy surrounding the Wizard and reported that it was, in reality, only a bunch of financiers scheming to get rich.

As bubbles continued to burst, the illusions became more and more unlikely and the attempts to sustain the illusions became more frantic…more war, more threats, more need for surveillance.

And finally, a new voice was heard in the land. A voice not claiming to need financial Wizards. This voice spoke of what the people already had suspected. The voice told the people they could take back control of their lives and reclaim their resources. It told them that what had seemed to be reality was just an illusion and not only an illusion but a scam, a flimflam to bilk them out of their resources and destroy their democracy.

They could leave Oz and move back to their old lives in Democracy.

People responded to that message as it resonated with their perceptions of reality.

But in one last attempt to keep control, the Wizard pulled out all the stops to prevent the people from voting for that voice of reason and hope.

Finally, the Wizard and his ruling elite succeeded, and the election would only be between those who supported the principles of Oz.

Into that vacuum stepped the ultimate con-man, full of bluster and empty promises, controlling the media with outrageous actions, provocations, and promising changes in Oz.

16

All of the courtesans of Oz thought he couldn't possibly be elected, having great fun and making crude jokes about him.

He said he would repair the walls, buff up the illusions of Oz, identify the internal and external enemy

There were many, the courtesans and acolytes of Oz, those who had been most green, even the intellectuals of Oz who had explained the inevitability of Oz; those whose livelihoods depended on continuing the illusions of Oz, who wanted only to make minor changes in, what they saw, as a great system…perhaps just a new president?

He said he would repair the walls, buff up the illusions of Oz, identify the internal and external enemies and give them hell, and he provide all citizens new and better emerald glasses.

Then came the earthquake of the election. The impossible had happened, and now this new President with his Barnum and Bailey bluster, his crude and uncivil speech and actions were in charge of all the levers of power in the American Oz.

And change would indeed be coming.

Many were unhappy with how it all happened. They were aware of the emptiness of the illusions, and they realized they had been hoodwinked into allowing the Great Oz to run their lives and determine their futures. It had all worked out badly for them and many were ready to leave Oz.

And that brought us to this American Watershed moment.

With the election, the walls of the American Oz fell, forcing the last remnants of the illusion to crumble, letting in the realities of the world and exposing the raw power behind the illusion of Oz.

Would the people, with new glasses, simply follow the new Oz into an unsustainable dystopian future, or would they regain their courage as citizens and follow the different drummer of democracy once again, restoring their heritage and moving back to a sustainable future?

The final question is, after their stay in Oz, have they found their brain again, and their heart, and, mostly, their courage to stand up for themselves and for humanity?

Let us explore how this happened and more clearly identify the choices the people of Oz must make.

Saving Democracy-2025

The 2016 Presidential Election

A Tectonic Shift

We all watched the returns that night and realized that we were in the midst of a political earthquake. Like any other earthquake, it had transformed our environment, almost beyond recognition. We could still make out the basic forms and institutions, but we now saw them in a new light, transformed by the earthquake.

We were in the midst of radical transformation, everything seen with new clarity.

It is like the outer shells, the facades, of the institutions had collapsed, leaving the internal structures, now exposed. It was like people we thought we knew dropping their masks to reveal their true identity and their motives.

The illusions were suddenly gone, and we see what had always been there but had been hidden from us. It is like the science fiction movies where the human mask is taken off to reveal an alien life form beneath the surface.

Some had suspected the true nature of those institutions was different from what the surface seemed to indicate, and others had tried to tell us their true nature, only to be rejected as prophets of gloom and doom…conspiracy theorists…a term of opprobrium nearly as bad as being one who questioned free-market capitalism.

Nevertheless, we now were confronted with the naked truth about our trusted institutions and their realities as simply tools to manipulate us into supporting a system that had led to this earthquake.

The reasons this election worked out as it did have to do with systems which were no longer effective or relevant to

19

much of the electorate. They had been weakening for years and there were signs of that decay if one looked hard enough.

So, assuming that things were still as they had been in the past, the economic elite and the establishment they had carefully built, went about quietly anointing their chosen candidate for the upcoming election.

The Republican Party, the previous torch-bearer of the economic elite, was in disarray, having lost their discipline under pressure from their Tea Party element. That, in itself, was quite ironic since the Tea Party was formed to fight the racial war against the first black president and to stop, even the most benign liberal agenda items. Now the Republican Party found itself in total disarray, imploding under the sheer number of candidates attempting to run for President.

Meanwhile the Democratic National Committee (DNC) had been captured by the funding of the economic elite and had willingly joined the establishment, leaving their base behind if necessary.

Hillary was the epitome of the new Democrat. She was connected to all the levers of the power of the economic elite and willing to do their bidding. She had shown herself to be pro-war during her period as Secretary of State and was the ultimate insider with votes and funding all lined up.

The economic elite were willing to anoint her as their next presidential candidate with their funding and support. The Democratic Party was ready for the coronation in light of the disintegrating Republican Party. The bandwagon that had been started years ago, had followed the perfected and prescribed root and was now ready for its final march to the throne of power.

20

The Emperor Has No Clothes

And then the unthinkable happened, someone, Bernie Sanders, had the audacity to challenge the presumptive candidate of the Democratic Party and the assumed Queen of the economic elite establishment. Bernie Sanders was raining on her triumphal parade.

From the perspective of the economic elite this was not a real concern. He could never garner the media coverage and, most of all, would not have access to the funding from the economic elite. That alone should spell doom for any candidate according to the conventional wisdom of the establishment.

They assumed that Bernie was really no threat to the citadel of the establishment, even though this threat was really unforeseen and therefore they had no real defenses against such a threat.

What did happen was that the Bernie Sanders campaign spoke of all the weaknesses and flaws of the neoliberal economic model as it existed, to the real concerns and needs of the ordinary citizens and, finally, it put forward the possibility of real change that had, thus far, looked like it was an impossible option. So now there was, perhaps, a real place for those citizens who had felt so left out, to put their hope and their energy. There, perhaps, was an option to the "same-old, same-old".

Bernie was speaking to what Senator Paul Wellstone had called the Democratic Wing of the Democratic Party and it was beginning to soar on the previously untapped energy of the very people that had been the powerful base of the old Democratic Party, before it had gotten co-opted by the economic elite.

And then the conventional wisdom ended up not being true. There were such big crowds, such energy and, most of

21

all, real fund-raising strength outside of the establishment. Eventually, even the corporate mass media had to grudgingly begin to give the Sanders campaign some coverage.

The economic elite called in all their chips to try to discredit the Sanders campaign, but the crowds continued to grow as did the fund-raising. There was real momentum building and the inevitability of Hillary as the Democratic candidate was no longer a forgone conclusion and her establishment positions were being questioned.

She originally thought she was not going to really have to deal with issues in a walk-over of a disintegrating Republican Party, but now, her vulnerabilities had been exposed and some of her earlier baggage was also working against her. Besides all that, the polls were showing that Bernie would clearly be a stronger candidate against a Trump candidacy.

In spite of all that, the economic elite and their establishment saw the Sanders campaign as a real threat to the continuity of their domination with his talk of making fundamental changes to their system. So, calling in all their chits, they called upon the DNC to manipulate the Sanders campaign out of the running with inner-party technicalities.

In effect Hillary Clinton and the DNC shot down the soaring Democratic Wing of the Democratic Party, leaving many in the Democratic Party bloody and wounded, frustrated and angry. This is not even to mention the independents who were ready to join the fight.

They succeeded but the result was that the base of the traditional Democratic Party saw what was being done and understood why it was occurring. Enough of them were now disillusioned by what they saw as a betrayal, not to mention all of the independents who had responded to Bernie's message.

So now, in the process of using the DNC to stop the Sanders threat to neoliberal economics, the economic elite risked finding out it was really a pyrrhic victory.

But, not to worry, Hillary was running against Donald Trump. "You can't be serious about thinking she could lose." All of the insiders of Washington, all the talking heads and pundits, all the intellectuals, assured themselves and others that Hillary would definitely win. And, reminiscent of the Dewey-Truman election of 1948, they were absolutely wrong.

In the attempt to stop the Sanders campaign, the economic elite made this election an election between 2 candidates coming from within the ruling elite. One candidate, Hillary, clearly seen as simply continuing on the trajectory of the Obama years, which had been hurting most of the populace economically and who were feeling left out.

The Art of the Deal

Just as in his business dealing, Donald Trump was the ultimate wheeler-dealer, willing to say or do anything to make a deal to his benefit. In business it has often been said that there are no problems, only business opportunities.

He saw that the loss of support for the traditional established politics, the traditional political parties and the continuation of the "business as usual" approach to the nation's problems had opened up an opportunity that could be exploited. The success of the Bernie Sanders' campaign and extreme reaction of the DNC representing the economic elite showed him the power to be exploited in a populist appeal.

Without having to betray his own deep involvement in the successes of neoliberal economics, he saw that, if he tweaked the system a bit, he could present a new and popular version of that system that could translate into support and votes. If he came up short it would, at least, have given him exposure for his name and his brand which would surely translate into future profits.

What were the elements of the deal? First, he could tailor his message to appeal to the ordinary citizens and not to the out-of-fashion political establishment, the talking-heads, the intellectuals or to the political insiders to take advantage of the frustration and anger of an apparently empty and dysfunctional political system.

With abortion and gun control in the background, he could call upon the recent decisions about gay rights and gay marriage, the recent rise to power of a racial minority with the election of Barack Obama and the potential rise to power of a woman with the candidacy of Hilary Clinton to rally the socially conservative voters to oppose the inroads of "liberal politics". The American Care Act, negatively labeled as Obamacare, was a natural example of recent liberal legislation, and therefore a target.

By shifting the focus of neoliberal economics from a worldwide phenomenon to a focus on this nation, he could begin his "America First" and "Make America Great Again" campaigns, tapping into a strong impulse toward nationalism and American exceptionalism. He saw that it would be like giving everyone a cap that said, "We're Number One" and a foam hand with the first finger raised. With that he could drive the crowd into a frenzy.

He could stay true to his neoliberal economic roots by proclaiming that jobs were the answer to the nation's problems. If we could provide jobs all of the nation's ills would disappear. Not only that, he, as a successful businessman knew how to provide those jobs and had done it before. That, coupled with his disdain for multinational trade agreements made him a darling of many.

The next element was to link our national problems with certain groups that were causing the system not to work effectively. Here was the source for demonizing; if you are not with us, you are against us. Some of them were outside forces, terrorists, foreign nations and their desires, immigrants and those who thought they had better solutions, rejecting the precepts of American exceptionalism. On the home front there were minorities, those with different lifestyles and women and, of course, liberals, not to mention the Washington insiders, the intellectuals (including scientists) who thought they are so smart and have all the answers.

It was a polarizing message, but the nation was used to such polarity going back to Newt Gingrich with his willingness to shut down the nation to get his way.

It was a risky gambit, but it was worth the investment, and it could pay off really well.

Add that to a populace who had been wounded and frustrated by the very party who should have been representing their interests and who knew that they had no good choices left. They could vote to continue the slow carnage by voting for Hillary or they could not vote at all, or they could vote for Trump (any change was better than none).

Also, being a master at using the media, Trump dominated the news for several months using Hillary's baggage to his advantage, as well as exposing the clear weaknesses of the current establishment.

In spite of the earlier support of the economic elite for Hillary Clinton, the economic elite realized that, if need be, they could live with Donald Trump since he was a creation of neoliberal economics and was not really a threat to their continued control. His election might expose the raw power behind the neoliberal economic elite, but it was better than losing control of the economic system. The worst part was

25

that Trump was such a loose cannon…too unpredictable. There was no way to be sure they could control and direct him.

So, we found ourselves in an election with little energy except negative energy, with no candidates that people really wanted. This was the ultimate result of a weakened system trying to gin up popular energy in a populace who had lost faith in it.

So, this was a perfect storm. People were frustrated and angry, feeling left out and mostly indifferent to the political options provided by the dying system. The heat and friction of the nation was growing. Anything could happen and the unthinkable did.

Donald Trump won the presidency. The devastating moves of the DNR destroyed the unity of the Democratic Party, resuscitating the defunct Republican Party, and turning over Congress and the nation to that Party for at least 2 years.

The scene was set for the further dismantling of the remnants of democracy and allowing the consolidating of the new-economic model, while allowing civility and basic social norms to disintegrate.

The other result of the election was to consolidate the opposition to the neoliberal economic model and to rule by an economic elite. The Democrats had been schizophrenic about their support of Obama, wanting to support him because he was a Democratic president and appalled by his continuation of the wars, drones and targeted assassinations, lack of support for unions and the growing income inequality. Now that the true nature of neoliberal economics had been exposed, showing how institutionalized and entrenched the rule of the economic elite had become. The result was that the ordinary citizens had no options except to change the system or acquiesce to the role as subjects.

26

Finally, in its obsession to protect itself from the forces of democratic reform, the economic aristocracy turned the nation over to a self-centered CEO and radical right-wing interests. One only needs to check the stock market to see that the economic aristocracy can live with that reality.

This was an American political earthquake, clearly the results of tectonic changes in the society. It will be the American watershed moment resulting in a political change of direction or making no major change and excepting a dystopian and unsustainable future.

Perspective: King of the Hill

After the dust from the Earthquake had settled, we all saw that this election had been a King of the Hill (like the kids' game) kind of contest. It had been an in-house, in-the-family, kind of fight to see which family member would get to wear the robe and crown, hold the scepter and sit on the throne and be "the decider," for the next four years.

It had been a no-holds-barred family fight with name-calling, hair-pulling, kicking, scratching and rolling around on the floor.

It was actually quite uncomfortable, and even embarrassing, to watch, but finally one of the contestants got to be "king of the hill" and like "queen for a day" got to personally decide what everyone else had to do.

Context/Basics

Introduction

Context and perspective are often helpful in gaining insight into the dynamics of things.

Part of the context of this perspective and discussion assumes certain basic ideas about forms of governance and the role that economic structures play in how the governance works.

From that framework of governance and economics, a narrative is formed...a social paradigm...that becomes the basis for developing an establishment to formalize basic ideas and to build a structure to protect and expand the basic ideas and the outreach of the narrative, almost as a kind of communal "spell".

Perspective: Plate Tectonics

Let's talk about seismic events and plate tectonics as a way of revealing an alternate perspective.

Probably everyone has heard some mention or reference to tectonic plates and has some rudimentary knowledge of the surface of the earth being made up of several of those tectonic plates. Those plates are part of a living planet and are continually moving and shifting, although quite slowly in human terms. Where those plates meet, one of two things is occurring. First, there may be pressures as the two plates move away from each other to create rifts, or cracks which will eventually lead to the two splitting apart. The second possible occurrence is that one plate rises up above the other, often creating mountains, while the other plate is pushed

28

beneath it. As you might guess, these events create a lot of friction and heat strong enough to melt stone, and this energy is often released through earthquakes or cracks where volcanic events occur. In addition, when the friction between the two plates gets great enough, the tension is suddenly released, popping the plates into a new position and creating seismic activities, i.e., earthquakes.

Let's use this as an analogy, an earthquake, a seismic shift, of the social and political narratives of this nation within the last years, culminating in the election of Donald Trump.

First, let us think about the politics of this country, and perhaps the world, being made up of two primary plates; one being the more authoritarian and economically oriented plate of neoliberal economics and the other being the democratic plate, where most of the people of this nation reside and are more focused on the health and welfare of the populace.

Historically the economic plate has ridden up over the democratic plate, exploiting the populace and dominating it with its economic power. From time to time the pressures of that subduction need to be released.

In explanation, as the pressure increased on the ridge or fault where the political tectonic plates join, the first rumblings of change in the political landscape began to be felt over the last couple of decades. The incredible pressures that had been building from conservative, market-driven plates continued to override the more

29

moderate, but far larger, mass of the old democratizing plate.

As the pressures built, subduction occurred. Eventually the heat and friction caused a major disruption, and everything changed. It was this kind of earthquake that has changed the political landscape and reoriented our world.

In the place of the old recognizable world, much of which was built on an illusion of progress, safety and security for all citizens, we are left with a stark view of what was behind that illusion…the raw power of ruthless economic forces.

The earthquake had created a new, and clarifying, reality. It was because of the clashing tectonic plates; one plate being our democratic heritage, valuing the human voices and participation of the ordinary citizens and the other being that of a world of unfettered free-market capitalism, neoliberal economics.

Organizing

Society/Governance

Once a society reaches a certain size, it is important to decide how to organize and structure that society so that it does not devolve into chaos. Instead, it is necessary to make sure that certain needs and functions will be attended to in some organized and cooperative way to provide structure and efficiency to the society. The goal is stability, allowing movement toward a sustainable future.

Healthy societies are made up of healthy people. To keep people healthy, there must be a focus on attending to their needs and concerns as well as helping them understand how the system of cooperation works to assure the existence of society and their health and wellbeing.

The Continuum of Governance: Authoritarian/Democratic

Since time immemorial, there have been two basic ways of organizing society, either top down (authoritarian) or bottom up (democratic). Of course, there are all kinds of issues to deal with in each of them, but either those on top decide how things will work, or the general populace is valued and finds a way to make group decisions about their collective futures and the future of the society as a whole.

As governance in the real world takes shape, each can be placed on a continuum from monarchy or dictatorship on the authoritarian end to a complete democracy, in which the voices of all segments of the society are part of the decision-making, at the other end.

One disclaimer…often societies start out in the democratic direction, only to have a powerful leader or elite group take over and turn it into an authoritarian society. In

31

recent history we saw that happen in Russia and China under Communism (Communism is based on democratic principles in its pure form), in Germany and Italy before WWII, and it is threatening to take place now in America. You might also note that in South America and Central America, after a brief flirtation with democracy, the powerful forces of authoritarianism are taking over again (Brazil, Ecuador, Venezuela and even Mexico).

One way to think about governmental forms is to look at the perspective upon which that government is based. The narrower the perspective, the more authoritarian the form of governance is. Is the vision or perspective of governance…what should be done and how it should be done…based upon one person's perspective, a small group's perspective or is it based on a more inclusive perspective? The narrower the perspective, the more the direction and solutions will be imposed from above. The broader the base of perspectives becomes, the less the directions and solutions will feel like answers imposed from someone else's perspective of what life is or should be.

The result is that the more inclusive the governance, the more likely it will reflect the perspectives of multiple groups and not just one or a few. The thinking is that such governance increases the likelihood of finding workable solutions that actually solve the problems for multiple groups and not just a ruling elite. It also gives the ordinary citizens a stake in the outcomes and in the future of that society. They are emotionally and intellectually invested in the wellbeing of the nation.

Perspective: Hammers and Nails

Everyone has probably heard the saying that if you are a hammer, you are sure that all problems are like nails and require a hammer to solve them. That same kind of thinking applies to any single perspective. If you are a general in the military, all problems look like they need a military solution. If you are a lawyer, you see legal solutions. If you are an educator, you see education as the solution. If you are a social worker, you see social programs as the solution. If you are unemployed, good paying jobs are the solution. If you are in the medical profession, all problems are connected with improved healthcare. If you are a religious leader, all problems have spiritual solutions. If you are a scientist, all problems have a scientific solution. The technical sector is sure that problems can be solved with a new computer program or app. If you are a historian, all problems are because we don't understand history. If you are of a particular race or gender, all solutions look like they simply need more input from your perspective. If you are an economist or financier, all problems have economic solutions.

As you can see, all these perspectives, while individually helpful, cannot give a broad enough view of the problem to likely provide a workable and sustainable solution.

Just a quick look at world history indicates the dominance of authoritarian schemes. They are all premised on an assumption that a small aristocracy, be it economic, military,

33

intellectual, technical, religious or hereditary, will be the most effective way to govern. There is an arrogant and hubristic assumption that the ordinary people, "the mob," "the rabble," are incapable of leadership, decision-making or self-governance. It is a bit like thinking that what has worked for the aristocracy in the past will be the best way into the future.

Authoritarian governance has often been justified as being based on the will of God (divine right of kings in Medieval Europe) or Gods as in many other cultures. It has always looked for ways to find vehicles to justify itself, whether it is wealth or position as a ruling aristocracy.

Much, if not most, of world history is about authoritarian leaders who exploit their subjects or citizens to reach their self-ordained goals. The relationship between the ruling aristocracies and the ordinary people was, at best, paternalistic and, at worst, simply a matter of exploitation. They always relied on the work of the ordinary people to support and fund their governance and to man their armies. This was mostly a domestic concern but also included occupied territories and colonies.

In the Western World that base of ruling authority began to expand from monarchs and the landed aristocracy to begin to include the wealthy merchants and bankers.

Gradually that led to pressure to include the ordinary workers and even women, other races, religions and foreigners, with the democratic goal to include all citizens.

The reason that democracy is the best framework for sustainable human growth and development is because it provides a broader perspective…a stable structure…while valuing and respecting all of its citizens and providing equal voice, opportunity and basic fairness. With all voices represented there are opportunities for real, workable solutions to human problems while finding balance within diverse needs.

34

Democracy is so seductive in its appeal because it rejects the idea that the general populace is merely a mob or rabble, incapable of making rational decisions about the direction of their own lives, much less a nation. A democratic populace answers, "We are not a mob or rabble, but intelligent, mature, creative people with unique and important experiences and wisdom about life, and we have much to add to a previously narrow perspective on how to effectively find workable solutions to human problems".

The fundamental relationship between the government and the people being governed has changed in a democracy. All the people are now part of the system of governance. The basic principle of equality changes the relationship to one of equals from one of an elite being viewed as superior or more important. It demonstrates faith in ordinary people. It is a humanizing system, concerned primarily with the welfare of the people of the society.

In a democracy the government serves the people while in authoritarian systems, the people serve the government which represents the needs of those in control.

Authoritarian systems rely on the manipulation of life and reality to fit the ideology of those in authority and then to impose their solutions to human problems.

Perspective: The Seawall

One of the primary functions of a democratic government is to build, maintain and continue to improve a seawall around that democracy.

The purpose of that seawall is to keep the oceans of individual or corporate wealth and power from flooding in to drown democracy, inundating it and overwhelming it with concentrated wealth and power and turning it

35

into a government of an aristocracy of wealth and special influence.

If the existing government fails at its job or begins to encourage poking holes in that seawall and not maintaining the seawall, it becomes clear that it wants to destroy the seawall and change the nature of the governance for that society.

If while they are doing that, they can convince the populace that, like the little Dutch boy who saved Holland by putting his finger in the hole in the dyke until help could come, it is the job of individual citizens to find the leaks and holes in the seawall and do everything in their power to save the nation by stopping that particular leak.

The result is that you have groups of citizens, some small groups and some very large, dedicated to stopping a particular leak. The problem is that if the government is not supportive of the seawall in the first place, it is a losing fight.

Only by returning to a democracy, one that whole-heartedly believes in the importance and maintenance of that seawall is there any hope. Otherwise, it is like trying to sweep back the tides, a hopeless proposition, using up valuable resources and energy for no significant outcome, no matter how well-intended the actions,

If the governing aristocracy really has no desire to maintain that seawall, it is also overjoyed to see so many of its citizens using their time and energy to try to save the seawall instead of unifying to change the ruling

Saving Democracy-2025

system back to a democracy which would then rebuild and maintain the seawall.

Economic Systems

• Three Current Economic Systems

There are economic systems and there are systems of governance, and each system of governance needs to be supported by an economic system. The interesting thing is that only two of the economic systems, Communism and Socialism, are directly connected to a system of governance. Capitalism is not.

Communism as an economic system was intended to support a democratic form of government (the people's government), although in practice it often got stuck on the phase of the dictatorship of the proletariat and devolved into a more permanent dictatorship.

One observation…both Capitalism and Communism are attempts at engineered solutions to human society. Both are about opposing solutions, one with economic engineering and the other with social engineering, on a society of human beings. Their goal is to make that human society fit within the confines of a theory, philosophy or ideology. Even if it is successful in the short term, eventually it will need to comply with the realities of human existence.

The difference with democracy is that, as theory of governance, it is based on a living growing society of free people who choose their own way as they grow, develop and evolve. Instead of making the people fit the theory, the people define their own world and path as it evolves. Ultimately it is about having faith, and patience with the human process and

37

not needing to speed things up and to impose solutions that only thwart what is necessary for continued growth. Therein lies the creativity and surprise of human life.

Socialism is an economic system that also is intended to support democracy with a balance of public ownership and private ownership.

It is only Capitalism that is not connected with a system of governance, although it is most often linked to the American and European kinds of democracy. The initial goal in such systems was to be sure that Capitalism supported the needs of democracy.

Once Capitalism begins to overshadow democracy it becomes aware that democracy is not necessary for its success and it begins to dispense with the democratic impediments, and it soon dispenses with democracy itself, thus concentrating all wealth and control in the hands of an economic aristocracy or oligarchy.

The latest form of this kind of perversion of liberal capitalism is the misnamed neoliberal economics. It is hard to connect this with liberalism in any way. Neoliberal economics substitutes the changes of the financial markets as the decision-making tool for social policies, rather than concerning itself about the welfare of the citizens. These market changes can be, and often are, manipulated by those with market influence and inside information.

Ultimately nations are faced with a choice of priorities; will people or wealth be the priority. If the priority is the welfare of the citizens, then it follows that there must be an economic system to support Democracy. If the focus is on wealth and possessions, then economics take priority, and the trappings of social structure are there only to support that goal for the few at the expense of the many. Life is seen more as a commodity to be monetized and used to produce wealth.

In such a system, wealth becomes the beacon for the society. In a Democracy the beacon is hope for human welfare with its focus on the people and supporting the human spirit.

Democracy values a balance of governance and economics, which is necessary to keep the life of the planet and the lives of the people healthy and functioning in a balanced and sustainable way. It is simply more humanizing and supportive of the human spirit.

The ultimate question is whether it is sustainable to have a society based on a superior/inferior relationship between those who govern and those who are governed or is it necessary for everyone to be a part of the governing process as equals to allow the possibility of sustainability. And how can the economic system serve that end?

- **Work**

There are many kinds of work that people do in their ordinary lives. There is the work of surviving as an individual, growing and staying healthy; there is the work of developing and maintaining relationships and community that are important to a full and satisfying life; there is the work of maintaining a family; there is the work of maintaining a healthy relationship with the planet; there is the work to maintain a spiritual life; and finally there is the work to produce adequate income to function within the economics of life.

Working to make money, as you can see, is not the only kind of work that human beings do, but it is about how we prioritize working for economic gain, that separates economic systems. If this kind of work becomes the defining focus behind the value of a human being, then we produce a system like free-market capitalism. If, on the other hand, that work for economic gain is only part of the focus...resulting in placing a value on the other work and the other relationships of human life...then we have something more like socialism, or democracy, in which both kinds of work are valued and supported.

Working for economic gain is a complex issue. The person who desires financial gain must find a way to sell his/her strengths, skills, talents or gifts by finding a way to make what they have to offer, fit the need within the economic structure over which they exert little to no control. This may be devising a creative way of offering a service. Often it is finding an employer who might use what they have to offer.

This is about presenting yourself in ways that someone else wants you to be in exchange for financial gain. In the process, the worker loses a certain amount of control of his/her life needing to find ways to conform to someone else's idea of what he/she should be, often creating a conflict within the worker, especially when certain boundaries are crossed.

If survival is at stake there are hardly any limits to what a worker will tolerate. This puts all the manipulative powers in the hands of the employers and those who profit from them.

That, of course, is the impetus behind workers banding together to form unions to counterbalance the enormous power and control that owners and employers exert on that system of working for wages. Workers are attempting to exert some control over their economic lives.

- **Role of Government**

In an authoritarian system, the role of government is to support the goals of the ruling elite. In the other system…Democracy…the government's role is to support the citizens in all of the forms of work. In other words, there is a public side that supports citizens' health and well-being as human beings, and there is the public and private enterprise side that supports work for financial benefit.

- **Role of Citizens**

The role of citizens is very different in the two forms of governance. Are the citizens there to support the economic goals of a ruling elite, or is the economy there to support the well-being of the citizens and the government that supports that end?

- **The Narrative: The Paradigm**

The narrative for a society is the underlying story of how and why the structural choices are the logical and best choice for the society. It provides the emotional and intellectual basis for that society.

A paradigm is a worldview that underlies the narrative but also defines how a society views the world. It also defines how to proceed and live in that world. It provides the ideological underpinnings for the society.

Structuring Society

Building an Establishment

Once a ruling narrative has been selected, whether by open choice or by manipulation, that narrative begins to consolidate its power and to build a system to sustain itself. In that way it is like any other organization… and maintenance becomes a part of its structure.

If the new ruling group rises to power on the back of some different ideology or some different narrative for the society, then the work is often quicker and deeper than it would be if they were simply a continuation of an existing system.

If it is a major change, or even if it is simply taking another step on the ideological ladder, there is a process of changing some hearts and minds that accompanies the process. The new ruling group is also eager to piggyback on any trauma, event or occurrence that can be used to further their agenda. 9/11 was such an event for the establishment of the fundamentals of neoliberal economics, much as Naomi Klein outlined in her book, The Shock Doctrine.

It is like building a fortress to protect the inner core of the ideology upon which their power is built.

In political terms, the new establishment moves to influence, and hopefully, eventually dominate and control the levers of power within the society. This can be done in a variety of ways, some more open and democratic and some more subversive and manipulative, depending on the methods and goals of the new ideology.

One of the first places to start is with the electoral process. The goal is to eventually control the process in a somewhat predictable way so they can plan and carry out their programs to prove the validity of their ideology. This, of course, expands to include the state, county and local levels of politics.

42

High on the agenda is finding ways to influence and/or control economics. That means working with those who already have wealth as well as successful businesses and corporations, banks, Wall Street firms, and others in the financial industries. It also means developing tax codes to support the goals of their ideology and those who support them.

It also means finding ways to influence the intellectual base of the society as well as the influential institutions, including the arts and the philanthropic institutions.

And then there are the defensive concerns. How do they correct any perceived vulnerabilities and protect themselves against destructive attacks that might weaken their momentum?

The longer an ideology remains in power, the stronger and more effective its Establishment becomes. They begin to have greater and greater influence on the hearts and minds of the populace, on the legislative agenda, on the media, on the courts, on the presidency, on business and the economy, on government itself, on influential organizations and institutions, and even on education.

This simply becomes the conventional wisdom of how things should work and do work. They begin to control, not only the agenda, but the processes that allow that agenda to move forward.

They simply discredit or co-opt much of the potential opposition. They also develop the illusion that change can occur within the system if one uses the established paths to create change. In other words, they imply that change can come from within the belly of the beast. What does occur with this process is that the change agents are simply swallowed up, digested for their food value, and whatever is left, excreted.

The other discouraging thing is that, eventually the intellectual community becomes so co-opted that, although they may identify real problems and issues, they continue to insist that change can occur if you work really hard within the system's guidelines, thus dooming those who sincerely want change to burnout and frustration.

There are a myriad of ways to use existing mechanisms to move their programs forward and to present a positive image to the citizenry.

At their disposal is also the might of the government itself and all its agencies, as well as the intimidation of the justice system, the military and the security state, if they should choose to use them.

However, once the ideology ceases to deliver on its promises, or those promises are exposed to be shams to cover ulterior motives, the foundations of the establishment begin to crumble and the weaknesses are exposed, sapping its power and influence. That is often when the work to sustain the illusion of the ideology increases and, at times, fear, distraction and intimidation are used to obfuscate from those weaknesses.

There are even times when those in control would rather bring down the entire structure around their ears rather than allow significant change.

However, any change, any reformed government, any new narrative or paradigm will either adapt the old establishment to its purposes or build its own establishment with different dimensions.

Perspective: Learning to Spell

Think of life as a series of narratives, or spells, under which we tend to live. The secret is that we choose those spells either actively or tacitly, accepting the spells others tell us to accept.

One of the important lessons of life is the process of learning to spell.

Every paradigm, every narrative, every philosophy carries with it a spell. The spell is connected with buying into the belief system that supports and justifies those particular beliefs.

The power of a spell is that it becomes a part of who we are and therefore becomes part of the accepted explanation of reality. It is the set of assumptions that we take for granted. It becomes the conventional wisdom of a society.

Ultimately it is a good spell for an individual and a society if it moves that individual and the society forward in a positive and sustainable direction.

It is a bad spell when the individual, the society and humanity are moving in a negative direction resulting in more harm than good.

The difficulty is that spells are powerful, and therefore hard to break.

Most spells to which we succumb require us to relinquish some of our decision-making, our personal thought processes, your individuality and our personal empowerment. Of course, some of that is natural if you

45

are to join the community of believers. The problem is when it begins to look like there is no way to break away, even when you can see how you are being damaged by that system.

It is almost like that system has become the world, your reality, outside which nothing else can, or does, exist.

When that happens, you have fallen under the spell of a certain kind of victimhood. You have lost your volition to be empowered and are willing to accept a role of submissiveness.

There is another way you can succumb to the spell of victimhood. That is when some traumatic or life-changing event occurs from a source beyond your control.

In that moment your old life disappears, probably never to return. If you focus on that reality, all that is left is an emptiness where your life used to be. It may feel like evil or supernatural forces have stepped into your life to take your perfectly good life from you.

It is difficult not to want to place blame, find causes, and then to seek vengeance or punishment, or at least get recompense for what you lost.

The spell of victimhood is like creating a world within that spell, like the world inside those snow globes with a city inside. Victims often feel they are locked in that kind of bubble with the rest of the world outside and with no way to reconnect with it unless a knight on a charger breaks through with his or her lance.

What we find is that, although many may try, they can never quite break through, leaving us feeling betrayed and even more alone in our victimhood.

At some point, sometimes early on, sometimes later, we get tired of waiting to be saved and take matters into our own hands.

As soon as we try this, we begin to realize that the bubble becomes less stable and it is soon clear to us that, if we take charge of our own lives and choose to join the world, the bubble disappears.

This is a test of your spelling ability. Do you simply stay stuck in the old spell of your life, or do you choose an alternative?

The reality is that we had cast the spell of victimhood on ourselves because we felt so disempowered after the traumatic event and that as soon as we decided that joining life again was only a matter of giving up the hope of returning to our old life and redefining life under new circumstances. In other words, choosing to be empowered once again and taking charge of our own lives.

In fact, we had done this many times before in different circumstances. Our world changed when we learned to talk, or walk, or when we got married, got our first real job, had our first child or a myriad of other life-changing events. Our world also changed with the negative events of our lives, when we lost a job, when our relationships dissolved, when someone we cared for died, when we were betrayed or deceived, or when we found that what we deeply believed was not true.

47

All of those events required that we leave the old lives behind and build new ones. The good news is that we have had practice at this.

The key, of course, is that we chose empowerment and not disempowerment, life and not victimhood.

How We Got Here

Introduction

From the very beginning of our national history, there have been forces carefully, and often very effectively, working to limit the growth and spread of democracy. This has taken the form of a number of theories put forward to justify why democracy, and especially the right to vote, should not be afforded to everyone.

Here is a partial list of such theories.

Religious - Christianity was used as a justification to take the land of the "heathen" Native American Indians. It was used again to limit the acceptability of other religions such as Judaism, Islam and an assortment of Eastern religions. It even went so far as to exclude Catholicism for a while, i.e., the Ku Klux Klan was against Negroes, Jews and Catholics.

Ethnicity - White Anglo-Saxon Protestants (WASPs) were seen as the standard and many others were seen as inferior i.e. the Irish, the Southern Europeans, the Eastern Europeans, not to mention almost anyone from any of the other Continents.

Education/Intelligence/Class - This was a matter of not just formal education but also owning property or having social status…what might have been called "breeding".

Gender - Women were considered inferior to males and not allowed to vote, among other restrictions.

Other subjective measures:

Patriotism - How completely one accepted the direction of the administration that was in power at the time, without judgment. This was often tied to a total support of the military, without question.

Capitalism - How staunch and unquestioning was the support of the precepts of Capitalism, often measured by how complete the rejection of anything labeled Communist or Socialist was.

All of these theories were projected as a normal part of being an American and were, at times, nearly totally accepted by a majority of the citizens.

Add to that the influence of the economic aristocracy, present and influential since the beginning of this nation, after having nearly destroyed the country by the end of the 1920s, were deposed and replaced by a much more democratic version of this nation under FDR and the New Deal.

However, the economic elite continued to believe in their leadership and felt they were entitled to rule once again.

After FDR's death, they began to gradually reassert their power by limiting or discontinuing the New Deal policies, focusing especially on restricting labor unions. At first the Cold War was presented as an ongoing power struggle with Russia and Communism, providing a vehicle for their return to power with its concentration on a military build-up and corporate involvement, pretty much with an open checkbook from the public.

As that elite began to regain power, they began to infiltrate government and institutions, often capturing or subverting oversight and the regulatory agencies. Once they became powerful enough, they began to work the political process to insert their alien economic ideology as a replacement for democracy. This was done very subtly, and most people continued to assume they were still operating under the old rules… if you worked hard and played by the rules, you would come out OK.

The new ideology developed a narrative, an illusion, that everyone could be prosperous with a secure future if they just turned the control of the finances of the nation over to an economic elite. This was very seductive, and a great majority

50

of Americans believed it and gave that economic elite their money and control of the government.

Around the beginning of the 1970s, with a renewed focus on law and order, the democratizing voices were suppressed and gradually quieted. Foreign policy was now firmly in the control of the ruling administration with less and less public voice, and secrecy became the watchword.

The focus, for ordinary citizens, was shifted from national purpose and involvement to a more personal purpose of acquisition and consumption with a more self-indulgent direction taking shape. We were encouraged to be consumers and to buy, buy, buy. Shopping became the national pastime and big box stores and malls began to spring up to meet that need. Credit cards became the method of purchase, and homes were a source of additional income with home equity loans, tying everyone to an economic system controlled by the economic elite.

If there were any funds left after the shopping spree, you were to invest it with the financial elite.

The sense of community was being dismantled with this economic focus and the American soul, our sense of building a human society, was being sold off.

Manipulative careers were in full vogue--banking and financial services, technology and business and management-- now manipulating and hollowing out American corporations. And government followed that same lead.

In time it became clear that the system was not really working as promised and that the economic elite were doing very well, but, at everyone else's expense.

Faith began to fade, but there did not seem to be any real options within the system.

The Bernie Sanders campaign provided a message that the system was rigged and that we had to change that system and move back to democracy once again. That message resonated with the realities of most of the American public.

Then the established power of the economic elite stepped in to derail that voice and that message, leaving only choices from within that system as options for the voting public.

The result was the farcical election of 2016 which caused an American social and political earthquake, exposing the establishment of the economic elite for what it was and leaving the nation under the control of extreme leadership.

This was an existential moment in America and will be seen, in the future, as a watershed moment when the nation chose the direction of its future.

Perspective: Town, Castle, Temple and Wall
The Town

Once upon a time there was a town. It was not a large town. It was not a particularly prosperous town, but it was a happy town in which people did their work, willingly cooperating when cooperation was necessary and felt good about their lives and their families.

There were differences at times, but the general neighborliness of the community tended to smooth things over, allowing people to agree to disagree.

When it came to decision-making, the town had a council made up of representatives of different elements of the community, the workers, the farmers, the businesses, the public workers and the general citizens. They all took their responsibilities very seriously and had many meetings with their constituents to be sure they understood and accurately represented the will of the people.

Somehow, they were always able to find solutions to their problems that were acceptable and that worked for the community.

It was not a perfect town, but it worked quite well, and the people were happy.

As time went by and the town continued to grow, some of the citizens, mostly the successful businessmen and some of the more prosperous farmers, suggested that the town build a new community meeting hall on the edge of town where new development was beginning. There were plans for a new business district, new factories, some new housing for workers and, on the hills behind the new development, the more prosperous community leaders were beginning to build houses and create parks. There was also ample space for community buildings…the perfect place for their new community meeting hall. One of the prosperous farmers said he would donate the land, and the businesspeople said they would pay for half of the building costs.

A group of businesspeople hired an architect, and the construction began after those plans were accepted by the community.

Some in the community were a little nervous about how this was all working, but the cost savings allayed their concerns.

Instead of a large open area for public meetings that the old town hall had, those plans had a smaller public meeting area and many small private offices. The town was told that this is how all such facilities were being built now.

53

So, the citizens were now divided up depending on the issue they were pursuing. A sense of community was lost in the process. But supposedly this new system was more efficient.

Eventually all the public, cultural and civic institutions began to move to the area near the community hall and more of the workers moved to be near the new business district and the factories.

Soon there were mines opened, lumbering was booming, and roads and railroads were being built in the new section while the old section of town was deteriorating. Since it represented the less economically focused past, it was hard to get funding for its upkeep. It began to nearly be forgotten.

Except for the area around the big new homes and the civic buildings, much of the land was being stripped of its natural cover and began to look lifeless and played out, but that only led to more expansion into new areas.

There was little thought about what that expansion was doing to the plants and wild-life, to the water or the air. Everything was booming and there was no sign of it stopping. There were occasional cave-ins, some streams were no longer good for fishing and the hunting was pretty much finished near town. There were also some mud slides and some hints of earthquakes, not seen in this area for hundreds of years.

The Castle

Work on the Castle had begun before almost anything else. The people learned that the plans had been made many years earlier. The Castle was to be the place where the Magistrate and his ministers would plan out how the town would be administered.

The Castle was an elaborate design with an outer wall, and some said, a plan for a moat and drawbridge.

The interior was very expensively appointed, some of it with private funds from the wealthy elite of the town.

There were large and small rooms for decision-making, and, as any castle would have, there were supposedly secret passages and ways to observe what was going on in any of the rooms. There were living quarters on the upper levels for the magistrate and his family. And, of course, there was a banquet room and a ballroom. There was also a huge kitchen and a staff to take care of the kitchen, the buildings, the events and the grounds.

The room in which the Magistrate received people was large and imposing. He sat on a raised platform in an imposing chair at one end of the room and those who were summoned entered at the other end and walked across the room to face the Magistrate.

It was a building exuding authority and awe.

The Temple

In the very center of the civic area, an area that had been open for several years now, the people began to see the construction of a new edifice. As people became curious, they were told that the business community was building a Temple of Commerce. It would be large and visible for miles around, with steeples and towers, almost church-like, but bigger, with a green light like a beacon on the top of it.

This would be where the secret and arcane plans would be made for how to maintain the progress and profits for the community. Only the top businesspeople, the academics and intellectuals who developed the theories and ideologies and the select politicians would devise the plans for how to sustain and spread the ideas which had been so successful for this community.

This was also the building that housed the police, the security agencies and the headquarters for the army, with an armory.

The Wall

One morning people were surprised to see the beginnings of a wall around that central area near the community hall but including the houses of the wealthiest citizens.

They were told that this wall was to protect against those who would try to steal the wealth of the community. Since that wealth was now considerable, the people could imagine the possibility of others becoming jealous and trying to steal that wealth.

The people were also told that security was needed at the walls...guards, police, perhaps even a military presence, powerful weapons, and even dogs.

They were also told that, in order to find potential threats beforehand, there was a need for security services, people who would secretly search out possible problems and analyze them to determine what, if any, actions would be required to thwart them.

This, of course, would all have to be secret, involving only those in the highest levels of the Castle and those in the Temple of Commerce.

The people were assured that this was for their protection and that the new surveillance technology that monitored their actions, their movements, and their communications--was only to find those who were trying to infiltrate the community and cause harm.

There were some apparent threats that had been thwarted, but it became clear that they had to step up the security within the wall. Instead of a free flow of people in and out of the wall, there would now be guards with guns and dogs at every gate, and that the citizens would have to produce identification to go in or out.

When there were civic meetings, elections or even some cultural events, the security became very intense, often causing long lines and long waits.

Eventually that complexity resulted in most of the community decisions being made by those within the wall.

In order to pay for all of this, the people were told wages would have to be cut and taxes would have to be raised.

Some disgruntled citizens even began to say that the wall was really about protecting the wealth of those inside the wall, not only from foreign threats, but from the citizens of the community too. They said this was simply walling in the wealth and walling out the people.

A Brief History of America

Constituting America/Early History

The most significant element of forming this new nation out of the English colonies, was that of the principle of democracy. It was certainly not perfect and had incredible exclusions, but the principle was established, much to the disbelief of the rest of the world and chagrin of some, since it spelled the beginning of the end of monarchy in Europe. It identified the yearning of ordinary people to be free to participate in their own governance…to have a voice in their lives and their futures.

And that has made all the difference!

The actual history of those early years was, as you might guess, a continual struggle between the desire of those with money and power to rule, as opposed to, continuing with a democracy, even in its early and restricted forms. More often than not, money won, but democracy stayed alive in the hearts and minds of the ordinary citizens as an inspiration and goal.

Whenever there was a national problem, especially involving foreign threat, the involvement of the entire population was necessary, and the ideals of democracy were called up and lauded.

Some of the pressure of this conflict was ameliorated by the availability of a frontier…open land (taken from the indigenous inhabitants) for escape and settlement, temporarily away from much of the control of the economic elite.

Unfortunately, after the new settlers did the hard work of establishing communities and enterprises, the economic elite soon followed to requisition them by fair or unfair means.

From the Civil War to the 1920s

The Civil War was partially a war about differing economic systems...the North being more into industrial development and paid labor, as a result of a large pool of immigrant labor to be exploited at very low wages, and the South with its more aristocratic plantation system with a seemingly endless supply of slave labor. This also meant that the southern aristocracy had total control of a huge segment of the population who had no vote and no real means of resisting their leadership. Besides this, slavery kept the cost of paid labor very low for the rest of the South.

The North won the war and slave labor was abolished, and throughout the nation immigration continued to provide cheap and exploitable labor to open up whole new areas of the nation. The side effect was a dominance of business and money with the huge fortunes to be amassed with the expansion of the railroads, timber, and oil, just to name a few.

Although African-Americans were partially integrated into the system they still existed more as second-class citizens than as anything near equals in our democracy.

Again, some democratic progress is made, but business comes to dominate again with the Gilded Age and the Robber Barons.

Rumblings from the ordinary citizens began to arise with the muckrakers (early investigative journalists and authors) who documented some of the most outrageous examples of social, economic and political abuses. (That was well before most of the media were controlled by corporations, although some were, even then.)

Eventually we had the phenomenon of Teddy Roosevelt who came to power after a presidential assassination (another American tradition). He extended the American Empire globally but did insist on some kind of fair play in the economic sector with his push against corruption and his "trust-busting" ...definitely a move toward an expanded sense of democracy.

Women were clamoring for inclusion and there were continuing attempts at unionizing workers to improve wages and working conditions which, up to then, were controlled by the employers and were more a function of profit than any concern for the welfare of the workers.

Industrialization continues and with Wilson's deal to allow the development of the Federal Reserve system allowing a cartel of private banks to control the money supply, the financial elite were again in the driver's seat by the end of the 1920s...and they drove the nation and the world right off the financial cliff.

From the New Deal to the End of the 20th Century

Then FDR entered the scene, and the New Deal was developed to save democracy from the clutches of an out-of-control economic elite.

He developed governmental programs to stabilize the banks and the economy. The New Deal developed programs to create jobs to put people back to work, to stimulate the economy and to protect people from the ravages of an uncontrolled economic elite.

Basically, he invited the citizens of the nation back into the governance of the nation by curtailing the influence of the economic elite.

If you had been born around the time of World War II, you experienced a society that worked as a community to win a war on several fronts and champion the democratizing impulses that have been so connected with the American Experience. Ordinary people volunteered to fight and to serve the war effort at home. It was a time of a very inclusive effort;

61

even the sons and daughters of the wealthy often joined in. Black Americans, American Indians, Hispanic Americans and even the interned Japanese-Americans served in the military and helped the war effort in every way they were allowed. Women became an important part of the war effort in the military and the factories as well as at home.

The unions were a significant part of the process, putting the needs of the nation above their personal needs...perhaps most clearly demonstrated by the merchant marines who manned the cargo ships that became the prey of the German U-Boats.

It was a time of saving scarce items for the war effort--of sacrifice, rationing, and victory gardens...but we knew we were all in it together, even the children.

Of course, there were those who profited greatly from the war itself and served more self-centered ends, but they were not encouraged or celebrated by any outside their inner circles. It was a time when democracy, community, service and citizenship were the most significant and serious concepts. These were the defining ideals of America, and we were rightly proud of them and willing to fight for them. It is in this context that the "Greatest Generation" comes to life.

The war ended and we were all relieved and happy about the victory with full recognition of the sacrifices that were made to achieve it.

Business and unionized workers thrived together. Prosperity spread. The GI Bill opened college doors to many who would not otherwise be able to get that kind of education and that, with the unions, formed a prosperous middle class...the envy of the rest of the world and the heart of American social and economic stability.

There was a social and economic safety net with unemployment insurance and Social Security. The government reflected the will of the ordinary people by providing programs for those who were disadvantaged or needed assistance. We were, in many ways, living by the precepts of a democracy, valuing our citizens.

There were, of course, those who were still pretty much left out. Racial minorities who returned to a very racist society after serving in the war found they were still excluded and that their service had little or no value in the eyes of others.

Women, who had filled many of the factory jobs, were now expected to go back to the home and allow the men to take their jobs back.

Once a person has clearly provided value in a society it hardly ever works for them to simply be willing to be devalued as though nothing has changed, not to mention their loss of economic independence. That, on top of the knowledge that they had always been treated as second- or third-class citizens and often not even as citizens. It appeared that they were simply to be willing to be exploited in times of need and then to willingly disappear into the background again when that need no longer existed...an incredible clash with the purported democratic ideals.

During the late 40's and the 50's public elementary and secondary schools taught their students about the evils of authoritarian government and how different and lucky we were to live in a democracy with the Constitution and Bill of Rights that protected them from such things. Totalitarianism and authoritarian governance were a threat to everything we held dear since they did not allow or reflect the involvement of the ordinary citizens in major decisions, nor did it reflect the will of the citizens, but instead, the vision of a small group who take it upon themselves to decide what is good for the nation and the people (mostly for themselves first). It was seen as a system that was based on arrogance and entitlement...one in which those in power see themselves as above the laws and rules that others must live by and above accountability, and thus, above question.

We learned that the way authoritarian governments retained power was through propaganda, militarism and a police and surveillance state to control activities, ideas and thoughts. There was always control of what people could see or read and propaganda was pervasive with control of all media. In those places all institutions were co-opted to serve that state vision, and the experts, intellectuals, and academics were also to serve the ends of the state. Information was censored, controlled and manipulated to serve the ends of the ruling group.

The laws, courts and prisons were used to serve these same ends. There were secret police and death squads to eliminate opposition and secret prisons and torture.

Everyone feared being labeled as an enemy of the state, which could happen at any time without warning and end life as they had known it. It didn't matter whether it was true or not, once in that category they were pretty much beyond hope.

Most American citizens felt safe and lucky to have all the protections a Constitutional Democracy affords.

Most citizens understood that authoritarian governments could exist from the more conservative side as in Hitler's Germany, Mussolini's Italy and Hirohito's Japan, or they could come from the other side as in "the dictatorships of the people" in Stalin's Russia and Mao's China. Those systems were all quickly perverted to be about the desire for control by a small group rather than the justification to achieve that end.

But the forces of the economic aristocracy had been hard at work trying to reestablish their power base even during the FDR administration. They were waiting for their opportunity and the period of relaxation at the end of World War II provided such an opportunity. The more conservative and business-oriented part of the Democratic Party found a way to manipulate the 1944 Democratic Convention to subvert the candidacy of Henry Wallace, who was enormously popular across the country, to continue as Vice President and to put a conservative candidate, Harry Truman, in his place in a coup at the convention. Truman was in politics through the support of Tom Prendergast in Missouri, a conservative power broker.

The conservative forces wanted to reign in the growing power of unions, i.e., workers, and to begin to reestablish the dominance of business and corporate control. They saw Russian Communism as more of a threat to their goals than the Nazis had ever been and with the momentum of the conservative, Winston Churchill, in England, Truman voiced this anti-communist concern. The result was the beginning of the Cold War, with Truman refusing to trust the Russians and his willingness to turn his back on any of the agreements that FDR had made.

It is important to remember that Russia had been the most important part of winning WWII for the allies and had suffered incredible losses in the process.

Russia had been under threat from the West since their inception and wanted a buffer (Eastern Europe) to protect themselves after the war. The tradeoff was for Russia to allow the reintroduction of a monarchy in Greece to come back to power to please England and protect its use of the Mediterranean as a route to the Suez Canal.

Russia upheld its part; but Truman would not even talk to them and Russia felt betrayed and thus the Cold War had been manufactured. It allowed our demonizing of communism and eventually socialism and even unions and workers and also allowed us to justify spending enormous amounts on the military to face the Russian "threat". This led to wars,

65

beginning with Korea, and other skirmishes during the ensuing years and began the slow march back to business and corporate dominance.

We, here in the US, also had those who would impose a kind of thought control, censorship and a test of orthodoxy with those who did not measure up, seen as heretics and Un-American. This was McCarthyism. We survived that threat, and the democratizing influences moved forward as did our prosperity.

This was a time of movement toward a more inclusive democracy led, in part, by JFK, and by Martin Luther King, Jr., and Robert Kennedy, all of whom had been assassinated by 1968. There were also the beginnings of student movements questioning established power in Europe and other parts of the world

During this time the War in Viet Nam began to pull us in. This was not like World War II. There was no military threat to us as a nation. The war was about stopping a treaty process from moving forward. When the French left what had been a French colony, Viet Nam was temporarily divided, to be reunited by an election to choose a leader for the entire country. Ho Chi Minh, whom the Vietnamese viewed as the equivalent of our George Washington, was clearly going to be the victor. The US did not consider him to be pro-Western enough and, so, wanted to prevent the election and impose a pro-Western leader on the country. All this is justified by the theory of the "domino effect" of Communism.

The hearts of the people in South Viet Nam were not really in the conflict and their leadership was corrupt so our efforts found only mixed support in South Vietnam. It became clear that we had neither the moral high ground, nor enough local support to do anything but impose our will on the country. In that situation both the leadership and the soldiers

66

on the ground were left in a kind of moral limbo that eventually allowed for any behavior that seemed to serve our policy ends, and that took a terrible toll on the psyches of those involved and on the entire society.

The propaganda became more and more transparent, and all involved were traumatized with the exposure of the illusion. We had spent untold amounts in lives and dollars, not to mention the environmental and social damage.

We did not want to acknowledge that it was an unwinnable proposition…in other words, admit defeat. So, we declared victory and left.

So, at the same time as the impulses of democracy were very active, those who had been in control traditionally were feeling threatened and also feeling that their "manhood" had been challenged.

So, Johnson, who pushed through the Civil Rights legislation, pursued the war as if it was a test of his, and by extension, the nation's, manhood and macho credibility in the world. He withdrew from the 1968 election because of the lack of support for his war policies and even sabotages Humphrey's candidacy by not allowing him to propose a way out until it was much too late.

By this time Martin Luther King Jr. had been assassinated, followed by great unrest in the Black community and later Bobby Kennedy is assassinated. In early 1970s the student killings at Kent State happened and established power clearly felt threatened and began to confront the democratizing elements…calling them Hippy, Un-American, Communist or Socialist…in other words, demonizing them.

The clearest confrontation came in Chicago outside the Democratic National Convention in 1968. Now established power took its position in opposition to the democratizing influences with the catch phrase, "Law and Order".

From here on the march toward a more authoritarian government became quite relentless.

Nixon promised he had a plan to end the war, and actually had Kissinger torpedo peace talks so he could win the election. He did not have a plan to end the war, and it dragged on for several more years with more death and destruction and a horrible price in terms of the national psyche.

The experience of the war in Vietnam left indelible scars on America. It exposed the systemic flaws in the basic governance of the nation. It exposed the prevalence of government lying and cover-ups in the administrations of both political parties. It showed the overarching power of political positioning. It also showed the problems involved in too much focus on a single article of faith such as stopping the spread of Communism at all costs and trying to make all issues fit into that concept. All of this supported polices to bring back rule by the economic elite.

It also showed the limitations of trying to engineer solutions to problems in other nations and the world. The final result of the war in Vietnam was exactly what would have naturally happened if we had simply stepped back and let events proceed according to the treaty that would have united Vietnam under Ho Chi Minh without all those years of death and destruction to reach that same end.

Under Nixon we watch the pullback begin with his policy of "Benign Neglect" for Blacks. He froze wages but not management pay. He developed an "Enemies List". He tried to corrupt the entire electoral process and succeeds in the 1972 election and was exposed as Watergate comes to light with the corruption that was involved.

He is forced to resign but his Republican replacement, Gerald Ford, pardons him, for what some saw as close to treasonous actions. (Just a note, Gerald Ford was never

68

elected to any office except by a small, conservative populace in a part of Michigan around Grand Rapids)

Remember that Agnew, Nixon's Vice President, had already resigned, charged with corruption and pleading Nolo Contendere.

After that, we have a brief respite under Carter, but he is undone after one term by the Iran hostage standoff with the Reagan campaign undermining a solution in order to win the election.

Now the reactionary changes began in earnest. The CIA and other American interests undermined governments in South America and Central America that had begun to give a voice to the majority indigenous populations. This nation supported death squads, arms for drugs, coups and assassinations to reimpose right wing dictatorships in that area.

Domestically there was a return to massive corruption, the Savings and Loan scandals, the beginning of the attack on unions with the Air Traffic Controllers, the "smoke and mirrors" of supply-side economics with its supposed "trickle down" effects, the tax breaks for the wealthy, the attacks on oversight, regulation and control, the incredible defense spending on things like the "Star Wars" program that never worked and a concomitant incredible increase in deficit spending.

By now wages had begun to flatten out and more and more of the increases in worker productivity were going to those on top, not to the workers or the rest of society.

Special interests and lobbyists are having a field day, and it all continues under George Bush I.

The other gradual change that had occurred was a shift from concern for democracy and the welfare of all the citizens to a more self-centered, consumer-based focus which comes to the fore. With economics being the focus, shopping became

69

that national pastime, malls sprang up, credit cards were king and home equity loans fueled the new consumer society. It was supported by a very well-developed advertising industry and the rise of financial institutions and financial advisors. Financial manipulation became more important than actually producing things. Citizens were being told what to think, what to buy, and not to worry their pretty little heads over the state of the nation or the foreign policies we, as a nation, were pursuing. Leave those to the experts.

We conveniently forgot that all of this was being done in our name and on our dime. We were funding the whole thing.

The result was a hollowing out of the American heritage and soul and the resulting attempt to fill that void with accumulating things, becoming more self-indulgent and seeing it as an entitlement and attempts to escape with drugs and sex. Eventually that emptiness turned to conflict and violence within the society, polarizing into factions, fighting each other instead of seeing the emptiness of the economic system that had been imposed upon their lives.

Finally, there is a break with Clinton, but he is under attack from the right wing almost from the beginning. However, he does make progress on many issues which help the ordinary citizens, and the middle class prospers.

Under continual pressure, he is eventually co-opted by the establishment economics in his second term, and we get welfare reform, pretty much within the Republican blueprint and eventually the repeal of the Glass-Steagall Act, which opens the field to all kinds of financial skullduggery, leading eventually to the debacle of 2008.

This was however, a very prosperous time and the deficit was erased, in fact there was a huge surplus of several billion dollars by the end of his administration.

The Twenty-first Century in America

When we reach the Twenty-First Century the economic elite is ready to dominate. They have honed and perfected their strategies and tactics and the final push to dismantle democracy is well underway.

George Bush II and Dick Cheney are elected in one of the most questionable elections in our history; it all was back on track in spades. He gave the surplus to the rich with a top-heavy tax reduction with the implied suggestion that part of this money be put into Republican reelection campaigns. He continued the policies of his Republican predecessors making them even more destructive to democracy.

After 9/11 his administration started its direct attack on the Constitution. He began two wars and allowed very loose and cavalier oversight. The result was that incredible amounts of money flowed freely without much supervision. These wars became profit streams for corporations and accomplished little. However, they cost the American society what was left of their moral high ground and what was left of the resources of the middle class. By now the wealth was all aggregated at the top and the deficit spending had nearly bankrupted us.

Then the economic conundrum of 2008 happened. The financial future of the middle class disappeared. More wealth moved up, the national debt was huge mostly because of the wars continuing to transfer wealth to the upper class. We were told that we must cut spending but that any new taxes were pretty much impossible even though those on top now controlled nearly all the wealth. In addition, those in the upper tax brackets saw their rates decreased by over 60% over the last 6 decades.

To finish the picture, we made torture, secret prisons, nearly universal surveillance, and indefinite detention a part of American life. We have death squads that roam the globe

71

doing targeted assassinations of those the president deems a threat. We have drones carrying out remote killings and our military is full of mercenaries, private contractors and specially trained killers.

Our military is posted in over 100 countries, and we have militarily segmented the world to have a command for each part of the globe. This is a modern version of imperialism.

Meanwhile the social structure as well as the physical infrastructure of the nation is deteriorating rapidly.

To make matters worse there has been a relentless attack on the structure and process of voting. The electoral system is being gamed, the voting machines are in private hands and money is the new determining voice in America, not to mention that corporations are now viewed as people with full citizens' rights.

The government has become so corrupted that it only serves the rich and powerful, the needs of corporations and financial institutions.

Ordinary people no longer have a voice.

It is within this context that Obama is elected with the real hope of the ordinary citizens that the economic debacle will provide a window of opportunity to reform the nation and realign us once again with our basic democratic beliefs.

After his election he dampened the excitement of a public ready to support reforms, suggesting that he had a plan and would work it out within government. However, the first part of his plan was to turn the economic elements of the government over to Wall Street professionals with his economic appointees, the very people who caused the problem and had a vested interest in protecting themselves, their former organizations and their friends.

From there it becomes a mixed bag. He makes some changes which the establishment can live with, but pretty much

72

plays by their rules. His health care priority is stripped of the public option and becomes a mandate to require all to purchase insurance, some of it subsidized by the taxpayers. The health insurance industry is left in charge of the health care in the nation which is like a ticking time bomb.

Nearly everything that Obama accomplishes in terms of democratic reforms is allowed by the economic elite and then used as wedge issues to polarize the nation. By the end of his administration, we have a nation polarized by gay marriage, by the Affordable Care Act, by issues concerning race, gender and immigration status. We still have massive military spending, with increasing use of drones and targeted assassinations.

In the midst of all of this we have continuing voter suppression, a policy of "too big to fail"/ "too big to jail" for financial institutions, the bailouts of corporations and financial institutions while the middle class is left to fend for itself with foreclosures and the results of the market debacle. All of this on our tax dollar. It is austerity to subsidize their prosperity. Meanwhile the wages and salaries of the ordinary citizens remain nearly stagnant.

This is not even to mention the lack of support for public education with his push for charter schools and privatization and his lack of support for unions and collective bargaining (he did not even visit Wisconsin in the midst of the destruction of public unions by Governor Walker). He did not even get involved as Michigan replaced publicly elected officials with appointed officials in Detroit, Flint, and Benton Harbor (all predominantly black) …a clear loss of democracy. We all saw the results of that with the water issues in Flint.

So, by the end of the Obama administration the trajectory remains clear for the bulk of the citizenry. They are being destroyed by continuation of the economic elite agenda

73

whether in its more blatant forms under Republican administrations or under its milder guise with the Democrats.

A majority of the citizens see that this is not a trajectory they can any longer survive. The neoliberal economic policies that had formed the heart of the Establishment are failing the people and they are insisting on change.

We were on the verge of a populist uprising.

Those of us who are old enough remember what we were taught all those years ago and realize that we have moved in an authoritarian direction and are well on our way to nearly all of those things we were told to fear and told that could never happen in this society. The elements of authoritarian rule seem to be rearing their heads in a nation that thought of itself as a democracy.

And all of this is what led up to the elections 2016 with its radical results that took us to another American Watershed moment.

The Economic Elite

Gaming the System

Gaming a system is probably as old as humankind. It has always been used to try to gain advantage by understanding the rules of a system and then figuring out how to use those rules for personal or business benefit in terms of financial gain or power. Even though the purpose of the system is clear, all that is significant to those who want to game it is how they can benefit. In the extreme it is like playing on the kindness of strangers to get them to stop for an accident in which someone appears to be hurt, only to find out that those who stopped you simply wanted to rob you.

The situation is seen in terms of a game in which there are winners and losers with the focus on being the winner. There is usually no concern of consequences or of collateral damage.

Vehicles to Support Dominance

Throughout our history the economic aristocracy has searched for and found various vehicles to support and justify their political dominance.

The first, and in some ways continuing, vehicle was to present economic stability as the preventative against foreign threats.

Next was to see that dominance as the means to develop the nation--i.e., such things as railroads, canals, energy, construction, the military, the navy, etc.

In many ways, we never left the war footing of WWII, always justifying secrecy and huge spending on the military and security services. First there was the threat of the USSR and the Cold War and after the fall of European communism, the threat of terrorism and the War on Terror.

This led to huge profits for the military-industrial complex and lately the security services. Even our foreign policy led to us being the weapons merchant for the world.

The economic elite saw the Russian Revolution as a real threat to the dominance of Capitalism as the reigning economic model. Anti-Communism became the rallying cry of the decades before WWII and grew even stronger after. The result was to weaken, and finally, nearly destroy, unions and to weaken citizens' organizations and a sense of a unified community.

After Communism faded, neoliberal economics became the vehicle of dominance.

We may, at this moment, be on the verge of the last of the neoliberal economic vehicle which will return the nation to a kind of feudalism, with a CEO as the king figure and the economic aristocracy as the support system, relegating the citizens to the role of peasants or serfs, working for the aristocracy in return for protection.

Neoliberal Economics as a Vehicle for Dominance

The economic elite are continually looking for means of justifying their right, or need, to be the ruling and decision-making group, best suited for governing a society. Because that requires the consent, at least the tacit consent, of a populace if they are willing to turn over their right to self-determination to such a group.

There is a long and successful history of such groups finding those justifications to keep popular support, often connected with perceived threats and national security. Neoliberal economics was a perfect vehicle to justify that domination again.

76

With its emphasis on economic results instead of human results, it shifted the focus of the society toward economic ends and promised personal and social prosperity if our destiny was turned over to them and to "market forces". This was to be accomplished through deregulation, privatization, and the concentration of capital at the top, linked to favorable tax codes and limiting spending for social programs. If we accomplished this, we would all prosper.

It also allowed the assumptions of the old American Dream to continue, at least in people's minds and perceptions. Many citizens continued to believe that the system was still fair and that, if they continued to work hard and play by the old rules, they would end up with a good life and a secure retirement.

It allowed them to continue to believe that the government was there to protect and support them and could be trusted to do so, that the same thing was true of the police, the military and the financial institutions.

On the surface the system continued to work for them, much as it did in the past, although the supporting system was being quietly changed to erode the very foundations of that version of the American Dream.

Perspective: An Alien Invasion

There had always been spores of this alien life form embedded in the societies of the Earth, but rarely had they found a culture that would support their growth. There had been periods where they grew and developed a pod of people who were taken under their spell. They had fed on life and the richness of human societies to grow a culture of economic zombies.

Those economic zombies had an insatiable need for any life forms, often even including natural resources, oil and gas, ores and, best of all, human intelligence.

Once in control they were able to get other humans to do their bidding, fearing that they might be devoured as food if they did not comply.

The economic zombies were also able to suck the human life out of some willing subjects, turning those erstwhile humans into economic zombies to join their ranks.

Their ultimate goal was to create an environment to support themselves by having a free hand to feed on existing life forms, the planet itself and, best of all, human beings, sucking the humanness out of them for their own nourishment. The result would be an entire race of aliens with no human concerns, only guided by their insatiable appetite to change life into wealth at any cost.

Once the economic zombies gained enough power, human concerns and any sense of human community practically disappeared, as did democracy with its concern for all participants within a society. What had been the human heart was replaced by a mechanistic ledger which kept economic score and assigned importance based on that score. Wealth became the blood supply in the circulatory system of the society. The brain was replaced by the insatiable need to consume life.

The larger that society of economic zombies grew, the more endangered, and less valued, the old-style human

78

life became. Soon the only options seemed to be doing the bidding of the economic zombies or letting them suck out your human brain and become one of them.

Soon the economic zombies had created an entire social structure and a set of established organizations and processes to support, expand, and continue their control and dominance.

But the existing human beings, seeing where things were going and what life under the economic zombies had in store for them, began to search for other options.

They began to realize that there had been other ways to run a society before this alien invasion, and it had been called democracy.

They began to realize that if they simply disconnected from the zombie culture and walked away, and back to democracy, the economic zombies would have little control over them, and they could begin to re-form a sustainable democratic life for themselves and for others who valued human society and wanted to return to a life based on those principles.

The economic zombies, incapable of understanding this kind of human logic, simply walked around in confusion as people began to leave their carefully constructed society for a "better place".

An Alien Ideology and a Quiet Coup: Mesmerized, Occupied and Preoccupied

- **Mesmerized**

79

The populace was simply mesmerized by the promises of a prosperous future as well as safety and security in what seemed to be a growing prosperity, especially during the 1990s. It was more like the "Pied Piper" mentality of trusting what the economic leaders were telling us and not really noticing where they were leading us.

- ## The Alien Ideology

Neoliberal economics was an alien ideology because it replaced the focus of democracy on people instead, focusing on economics and a kind of market morality...if it makes a profit, it is sound and if it doesn't make a profit, it should be discarded as bad policy, regardless of the human toll.

The alien ideology in its final form was neoliberal economics, with its primary proponent being Milton Friedman in the Reagan Administration in the 1980s. It is a system of allowing the markets to direct policy choices. In other words, let profitability direct government attention and action.

The new religion of neoliberal economics was built on a perversion of Adam Smith's Capitalism. It replaced the humanized heart of Democracy with a mechanistic heart of market morality. Market morality allowed business and government itself to turn over any need for responsible moral leadership to a mechanistic marketplace, allowing them to simply read the numbers produced by the market to know how to proceed. It was like reading the bones, or the dice, or the tea leaves and interpreting them to chart a course for the future. The big difference is that those who were reading the market were also in control and manipulating that market.

It was Adam Smith's "invisible hand of the marketplace" now belonging to the economic elite and reaching into the pockets of the unsuspecting populace to pick them clean.

The pretense was that if a nation becomes economically successful, all other social programs will be able to be funded

80

to take care of the common people. To get to this place, however, the nation must turn over its governance and the people must turn over their assets to those who control and understand how markets work. Once that is done, as the promise goes, we will have a prosperous, secure and sustainable future for the nation and for its citizens.

This is based on privatizing government functions and assets, getting rid of economic regulation and impediments, rewarding wealth accumulation by cutting taxes for the most successful, encouraging investments and defunding social services.

It is not hard to see that Democracy has little to no place in this formula, nor does the American Dream except to be used as a trapping to expand their power.

If you look at how government now works and which policies and programs gain ascendancy, you will see that the goals of neoliberal economics are firmly in control.

Governance may appear to be dysfunctional if viewed from the perspective of Democracy, but if viewed from the perspective of neoliberal economics it is extremely functional and quite successful.

The Quiet Coup

While we were distracted by the focus on outside threats, terrorism, Islamic fundamentalism, China, Russia, the Middle East, immigration, our wars; the economic elite were chipping away at democracy, changing the tax strategies and consolidating and securing their dominance with a myriad of inside changes to the structure of governance. They were busy discarding regulations and oversight, weakening or diminishing social programs. They were making life for most citizens less secure and more dependent on economic factors over which those citizens had little to no control.

Saving Democracy-2025

The future was increasingly based on individual economic success, regardless of any extenuating circumstances.

In addition, there was a continuous attack on voting rights, finding ways to control and limit voting with a variety of schemes.

The result was to greatly increase the gap between the economic elite and the rest of the society, taking down the middle class, the heart of our prosperity since the New Deal began. It was like tipping the table and watching the national resources roll into the pockets of the economic elite.

The process becomes quite evident. It is to transform life into wealth by taking the environment as well as human resources and changing the living, growing, interconnected systems into wealth with little to no regard for the death and destruction that occurs.

We have seen this process before, and we see it today. In the past it included things like hunting the buffalo to near extinction, clearcutting the forests, plowing up the prairie and then watching the topsoil blow away. This is not even to mention the destructiveness of mining on the environment. And finally, there is the extraction of fossil fuels, most recently fracking, resulting in the destructiveness to the natural environment, and serious changes in the global atmospheric conditions with the continual damage of carbon emissions.

All of this is justifiable within the structure of neoliberal economics since it produces increased wealth for an economic elite.

And with the extension of this ideology to much of the world it has become self-sustaining and dominant.

Preoccupied

By keeping the populace preoccupied with media sensationalism, celebrity gossip and scandal, with sports and the flash and dazzle of entertainment, with foreign adventures and threats, with wars and political drama, most people did not really notice that the American Dream was being undermined and replaced with a heartless mechanism of marketplace morality.

Perspective: Falling under the Spell: The New Religion

The Church of Wealth was constructed as part of a New World View, the view that was to provide salvation to all and the promise of paradise, if you had enough faith. With its beacon of Accumulated Wealth, it was seemingly available to all who followed the catechism of neoliberal economics and had faith in the priests of economic success.

The civic religion of democracy had been replaced by a new religion, and it required wholehearted conversion to the American Church of Wealth. Proof of faith was a willingness to invest in the future of that church. The expectation was that all would invest their resources in the Church, even being willing to be supported by a system of credit cards and loans from the Mother Church in order to make that commitment.

A new beacon replaced the beacon of democracy, which had guided the way with hope for a humanizing society and shared progress toward a sustainable future.

But wealth held such allure, and it had corrupting influence when it began to override all previous ethical and moral boundaries. It no longer seemed to matter that all other religions warned against just such corruption as did Democracy itself.

What had replaced the human heart behind that Democratic Beacon was a mechanistic and quite ruthless marketplace that required no individual responsibility and encouraged all parishioners to take care of themselves and those they cared about, and to allow the marketplace to take care of everyone else. It was ultimately a harsh and rigid religion.

In effect, the American Church of Wealth granted forgiveness and absolution and dealt heavily in indulgences for a price. The Church willingly took on the burden of sin and responsibility for its parishioners, assuring all that the Holy Spirit of the Financial Marketplace would reward those who were deserving and punish those who deserve to be punished. All you had to do was to watch who was doing well to know upon whom the Gods and High Priests of Wealth were looking favorably, and which others were being damned as unworthy. It was clear who to emulate.

The implications were clearly that the Prophets of Democracy were false prophets, now replaced with the true Prophets of Wealth and Profit.

Within every community, the Chambers of Commerce became the centers of the local Temples of Wealth. The Cathedrals of Wealth were the financial institutions and huge multi-national corporations. Those who ran those institutions were the High Priests of Wealth, and with the parish priests of the local Chambers of

Commerce, they continually recruited acolytes who were often richly rewarded for their services.

The beauty of the religion was that it was open every day, especially workdays, and you could worship on the job. Not only that, but there was a clear indicator of the success of the Church, displayed daily, such as the Dow Jones Average and other financial indicators.

The basic tenets of the new religion were repeated hundreds of times every day through advertising and propaganda.

The financial institutions continued to accumulate the personal resources of the populace, taking the lifeblood of the parishioners' economic life, and transforming it into wealth for those institutions.

But it is the corporations that are the real examples of how the new religion really worked. They took living resources and turned them into commodities (the only thing that had any real value in the new religion) and finally turning those living things, both natural and human, into wealth. Much like the Christian ideas of transforming water into a sacred wine, only now it is changing life into a dead abstraction, wealth. The only sacredness in that wealth is what is bestowed upon it by the high priests themselves.

But the allure of the paradise to follow the years of work and the continued financial support of the Church of Wealth was just too much to resist. Everyone was shown those who had become rich and successful by keeping the faith.

Anyone who had the timidity to question the teachings of the Church was quickly brought back into line by peer pressure and the intervention of the Church elders if need be. Those who openly questioned the foundations of the Church of Wealth were ostracized, publicly embarrassed, and, if need be, excommunicated. Blasphemy and heresy were definitely a part of the unspoken vocabulary.

To even suggest that the old civic religion of democracy was an alternative was to show how old and outdated your thinking was. This was a new world and required a new church, the Holy Church of Wealth.

There was no life and certainly no hope of salvation outside the Holy Church of Wealth.

Dehumanizing a Population

Once you replace the focus of concern for a healthy citizenry with an exclusive focus on wealth creation and economic growth, personal responsibility stops including others and simply becomes focusing on accumulating wealth. The human element necessary for a functioning democracy begins to fade and with it the cohesion of community and citizenship.

Replacing Democracy with Capitalism

The goal of neoliberal economics was to quietly replace the civic religion of this nation, displacing democracy and quietly replacing it with capitalism.

This was accomplished in several ways. First was to conflate democracy and capitalism so that, under the rubric of

Saving Democracy-2025

protecting or expanding Democracy we could really be protecting and expanding Capitalism. The economic elite knew that not many ordinary citizens would make sacrifices in the name of Capitalism alone, so it became a successful ruse.

Using the Establishment: Normalizing the Change

Part of the value of an establishment is that it provides a way to normalize changes, even major changes. If you can make the changes small and incremental, and not draw too much attention to them, all the changes will eventually be acceptable as "business as usual".

Changing the Rules: Institutionalizing the Change

The occupying ideology began to subtly impose the new paradigm, to change the rules, giving more power and influence on an economic elite and shifting the role of government away from helping the general citizenry, to funding and supporting the goals of an economic elite.

This was done by beginning to get rid of regulations for business. It was done with many small economic changes and some large changes like ending the Glass-Steagall Act and changing taxes to be more favorable to the economic elite.

Just a side note-in the 1950s, the upper tax brackets rates were 90% while currently they are about a third of that and even less for investment income. And still in the 1950s the rich were clearly rich, and everyone else knew they were rich, and the society was funded, and democracy was healthy, although not perfect. "Rich as Rockefeller" was a common saying.

Rules about unions were gradually changed weakening them and eventually it became open season for unrestricted money for political campaigns while voting restrictions began to be imposed and election tampering with voter suppression and voting machines.

Hollowing Out Democracy

As the focus shifts from the health of the citizens and the society to economic gain and power, not only are the corporations and governmental functions no longer benefitting ordinary citizens, but they are also taking the real heart and meaning out of the jobs, out of democracy and out of the nation, leaving only a cold and empty shell and a psychic emptiness in its place.

This leads to depression, attempts at escapism and, at times, to violence.

No people can remain healthy without meaning and heart to sustain them. No amount of wealth or accumulation of things will ever fill that void.

Engineered Solutions

With any system that is derived from a narrow perspective and a particular ideology with a set of working assumptions, there is a tendency to try to change the realities of life to fit with the assumptions of the ideology. The problem is that, when you are fighting the natural tendencies of life, those changes tend to be temporary at best and often do not work particularly well, giving a sense of artificiality to everything.

Engineered solutions are rarely lasting and often take things in directions that produce unexpected and negative consequences.

Those solutions almost always contain elements of arrogance and hubris and often require immense amounts of manipulation, resources, and energy.

Some indications of the level of manipulation during this period are apparent in the shift to manipulative careers — one example being the shift to the dominance of the financial industry, which is not about productive work, but about manipulating money. It is also reflected in the direction of politics with spin and campaign manipulations. It is also apparent in corporate management, managing often, hollowed-out businesses and corporations and off-shoring jobs and income to avoid taxes.

Proselytizing to the World: Globalization

As the neoliberal economic model began to define the world, several things happened. Through the significant influence of the World Bank and International Monetary Fund (IMF), the neoliberal model was imposed on many struggling or emerging nations, superseding their national governance and often destroying their local markets and thus their national production unless it was exportable-like natural resources, mining or oil.

This process threw their social structure into turmoil and thus their stability. They were told to privatize public resources and services and to repay the loans by cutting services and restructuring their economies to fit the neoliberal model.

The results were disastrous in many nations, although there was much money to be extracted in fairly conventional ways, or by vulture capitalists.

None of this was sustainable and, for most, there was little hope that things would improve.

The United States

Those same forces are working themselves out here in this nation.

While we were being distracted by the fears of outside threats, Capitalism was being conflated with democracy. So, if capitalism was being threatened by any democratizing movements in other nations, it was presented as a threat to democracy and "our way of life". "Our way of life" was becoming more and more unfettered free-market capitalism- and not really democracy at all.

Those perceived threats were also used to move Capitalism into a more dominant position with the military and security requirements of the Cold War and later the War on Terror.

Perspective: Hollowing Out/Mother Ship or Death Star

The concept of hollowing out is a process of taking the inner workings, the energy and life, the internal processes out of a structure or institution, leaving only the outer shell and the illusion that the structure is still alive and credible.

We have experienced much hollowing out over the last decades. The progressive tax system has been hollowed out to the extent that it is now more regressive than progressive. The military has been hollowed out, with most of the support functions now under the control of private companies, transforming them into profit streams for corporations while leaving the fighting and dying in the public sphere. Some of this has even been parceled out to lucrative private armies of mercenaries.

The process goes on apace with the State Department, the security agencies, as well as many public functions.

Saving Democracy-2025

This is also moving forward with the postal service and education.

The result of most of this hollowing out is to limit public control while keeping the public funding to make it profitable.

There is also the hollowing out in the private sector. Businesses and corporations have been hollowed out as their production, workforce, and profits have been offshored. The result is that the standards of living for workers and their families, as well as unions, have been hollowed out.

The final result is that the middle class, the basic realities of a democratic society, and democracy itself have all been hollowed out.

All that is left are empty shells.

All of this is a process of transferring public funds and subsidies into private hands while reducing public control, oversight, and regulation.

One might think about the process as emptying out the ideas from the material connections to a country or a political philosophy or even a planet. It is a way for things to exist in name only, or as a logo, or as a concept; untethered to any location, nationality or even any human identity.

It might be thought of as a mothership hovering in space and sending out craft to use the resources of the planet to fit its immediate needs, changing whenever those needs change and relocating above the planet to go wherever those resources might be most efficiently harvested.

The other picture would be that as a Death Star- here to use up the planet and its resources without any concern for human life or consequences. And if any should look like they might rebel, the Death Star would simply destroy that segment of the planet...or even the entire planet.

Corporations

In this process the role of corporations has become of significant importance. To begin with, corporations were financial abstractions to protect owners and investors from liability should the corporation run into trouble. They were to serve a public service and were chartered by a state with documents that controlled and limited their actions.

As corporations grew in size and influence and in their importance to creating and protecting wealth, their legal status began to grow and shift more toward benefitting the owners and investors than in any public function.

Due to some editing of a ruling sometime in the early twentieth century, the idea that they could be viewed as a person was added. This was eventually expanded to having the rights of a person but retaining the limits on liability, so they had rights but few ramifications if they abused those rights.

In the recent Citizens United ruling by a friendly Supreme Court, they were allowed to be viewed as a person with rights-with money as a means of speech-thus allowing unlimited funding of political speech.

One might think of modern multinational corporations as the powerful armored weapons with very limited liability, thus

Saving Democracy-2025

the "too big to fail" and "too big to jail" concepts of the Justice Department for financial institutions in the Obama administration.

They have, in effect, become weapons of mass destruction, gobbling up natural and human life and transforming it into wealth and leaving only its waste behind.

The behemoths have spread far beyond national borders-and thus beyond national control. They now exist as powerful entities with little limiting control of their desires. The result is multinational trade deals, accepted by nations to benefit corporate goals, with courts to adjudicate terms that supersede national laws, making them more like a ruling world government, almost like a death star, untethered from any human control.

This is like the Knights Templar of the Medieval Period, but without even the cover of altruistic goals.

Meanwhile the economic elite, in their continuing obsession with expanding their wealth, are protected by the legal armor the corporations provide.

Workers

Within this scenario, it is not hard to see the preferred role of workers. They are to be seen as a resource to be exploited and discarded. The pressure of businesses, corporations, and the economic elite has always been not only to limit wages, but also to curtail the rights of workers. They have consistently worked to pay the lowest wages possible without restriction and have been consistently opposed to any wage legislation including minimum wage laws. They have used many tactics to play workers off against each other with race, union vs. non-union workers, and low paying foreign workers.

Workers-since their only hope of countering the power of business and corporations was to band together to have

93

common goals-began to push for unions. This is an old desire and began to take a modern form in the early Twentieth Century, continuing on to its fruition in the New Deal, extending into the 1950s and 1960s.

Of course, the economic elite demonized Communism in Russia, seeing it as a direct threat to the dominance of Capitalism. In line with that thinking they made the argument that any groups, like unions, were really an example of the infiltration of Communistic ideas of communal action and therefore Un-American. Of course, they did not point out that their opposition to communal organization also undercut the sense of community at the heart of Democracy.

Shortly after the death of FDR, the business forces began to reform to begin to limit the rights of workers and unions. Later, with the Reagan administration, we saw the beginning of the end with his firing of the Air Traffic Controllers and the beginning of institutionalizing union busting.

We all know the results. As unions began to dwindle, so did the prosperity of the workers and thus the middle class.

Workers were once rewarded for increased productivity with raises and other benefits. Now wages are fixed and stagnant and productivity has been disconnected from wages. Workers are now expected to compete in the same field as low-paid foreign workers or lose those jobs overseas. Meanwhile they continue to lose their benefits and pensions, the results of years of negotiations.

Workers have been transformed from human beings deserving respect and dignity to being simply exploitable and replaceable economic units, to be discarded when they no longer have economic value within the system.

From Citizen to Subject or Mere Economic Units

The subtle transitions were slowly resulting in transforming the citizens of the nation into something more like subjects. Decision-making was concentrated in a small group of economic elites on the top and passed down, setting the framework within which the citizens must find a way to live.

Those citizens no longer had any direct voice nor any real representation and were left to respond to the vagaries of economics as best they could. They no longer had any real control of their lives or their futures and began to feel like simply exploitable resources rather than people.

Perspective: Addiction

One might think of great wealth as a drug that gives people a sense of power and dominance, a kind of high that can become addictive. Once addicted, like any other addiction, all bets are off and the single important goal is getting the next fix, in this case more wealth. Like any addiction, the fix is only temporary and needs to be continually renewed at all costs.

It is not hard to see, and we understand from our experiences with other addicts, that there is never enough, and it is never ending. The addicts are willing to sacrifice everything and everyone in their frantic search for the next fix. The result is that they leave a trail of chaos and destruction in their wake.

Media and Information: Propaganda and Censorship

What had once been a free press (although there always had been pressures from the economic elite) was soon consolidated and captured by corporations, turning it into an economic engine for profit and turning news into entertainment.

Another result of a corporate media was to turn a blind eye to anything that did not support the goals of the economic elite. The media finally turns out to be a platform for advertising and a propaganda tool, almost like a house organ.

However, many people still operate under the assumption that the media is still open and objective, so it continues to be an effective tool of the establishment.

Capturing the Political Parties and Government

Eventually, with the concentration of money in the hands of a small economic elite, and with tax codes supporting that process, money begins flooding into and controlling the political process with the Citizens United Supreme Court decision.

Soon both political parties become dependent on funding from the political elite to stay relevant and to have a chance of winning elections.

Protection and Predictability: Surveillance, Secrecy and Control

In order to control the complexities of ruling a diverse population predictability became paramount. If they were to protect and safeguard the integrity of the establishment, they needed to know what was going on so they could analyze the potential for threats and devise actions to prevent such threats from materializing.

96

To accomplish this, they would need a complex and seamless security system including information from complete surveillance and monitoring of people, as well as satellite monitoring from space, from the FBI, the CIA, the NSA, the military, from businesses and corporations, from ordinary people, and from politicians.

This system would, of course, need to be secret, only available to deep insiders.

Only in that way could you really protect the establishment.

Projecting Power: Wars and Trade

One way of not only spreading the neoliberal economic model but showing how powerful we were as a nation was through trade, making trade easiest for those who have adopted our economic model and punishing or exploiting those who didn't. So, trade deals became the currency of our power.

When things did not turn out as we wanted, when others balked at the imposition of our economic models and our power, our overwhelming military machine was in the wings ready for war to support our friends and defy our foes. It was a time for regime change and nation-building on the American Plan, according to the established powers.

The True Believers & The Collaborators

There are always great rewards for the true believers and the collaborators. They are granted special favors and given recognition and accolades. They are held up as the shining examples. Despite realities that seem to show that the program is not really working as advertised, they are counseling, "keep the faith" and "stay the course".

It goes without saying that those who choose to expose the system, the whistleblowers, are totally discredited and destroyed, their messages mostly ignored, except by those who suspected we were being manipulated.

They are sure they will eventually reap rewards for their loyalty. They do not realize they are the outliers and are considered quite expendable by the power brokers on the inside.

But, in the meantime, they feel noble and courageous as though they are the soldiers manning the front lines ready to defend the cause to the death.

Raw Power Exposed: Devolution to Authoritarianism

As the illusions begin to tatter, the true framework of the system is revealed to be the absolute power and control of the economic aristocracy. In the end the populace awakens to a world of authoritarian power and control, all of which has happened while they were distracted by the very powerful illusion of an economic paradise on earth.

The Beginning of the End: A Failing System

Introduction

As the façade begins to crack and fall away the failures of the social and political systems become apparent to more and more of the ordinary citizens.

The promises of prosperity and long-term security are clearly empty promises used to seduce the populace into sharing their financial resources with a financial industry run by the economic elite who were getting rich while everyone else was being left behind.

That economic elite was tap dancing as fast as it could to keep the populace investing in their schemes. We funded them with top-heavy tax breaks shortly after the beginning of the twenty-first century to signal that this was a Century they planned to own.

The emphasis was shifting rapidly from a government focused on helping the citizenry with social programs and infrastructure improvements, to a government used to strengthen the hold of the economic elite.

This was continued under the cover of the trauma of 9/11, and we were soon involved in two wars, terrorism threats and anti-Muslim sentiments. Tax money was thrown into every issue with little oversight or control, much of it disappearing into the yawning jaws of Iraq, supposedly to fund the war and rebuild the country, not to mention the funding of the Homeland Security agencies.

We all know how that turned out, what sacrifices the ordinary citizens made, how bankrupt the country was and how rich and powerful the economic elite were becoming.

Perspective: A Crumbling Edifice

The mortar that holds any system together is the faith and support of the ordinary people. When that faith and support wanes, the mortar begins to disintegrate and the structures-the edifices-of that system begin to be shaky and unstable. Even when that support is only tacit support the edifices are weakened.

When the edifice of neoliberal economics begins to lose the faith and support of the ordinary people of the world it begins to become shaky and crumble.

However, the inner sanctum of the system, the administrative system, stays intact and continues to be run by the high command and the true believers.

The outer protective walls remain intact and are manned by the soldiers and security agents of the system, now on high alert.

In an attempt to repair the shaky structures, those in command choose to substitute fear and even blood for the mortar of support to keep the edifice intact.

Parties Become Irrelevant

As the illusions of the Establishment become more and more threadbare, the political parties that have been co-opted to serve that establishment are seen as simply a means to move the establishment agenda forward and not any longer as being relevant to the needs of the ordinary citizens.

The result is that those parties begin to lose energy and weaken with the eventual outcome begin to be threatened by the voices of the populace.

To the degree that parties attend to this new energy, they may modify and survive, but they must decide whether to serve the establishment or the citizens of the nation. There is a real risk of losing the support and status of the Establishment if they decide to leave.

When the establishment has reigned for a long time, most of the politicians have become more like courtesans than representatives of their constituents.

Ignoring Popular Realities

The longer the establishment ignores the push of the popular realities, the more risk they run for confrontation and the more they turn to the tools of manipulation and intimidation. These include propaganda, indoctrination, the threat of force from police or the military, and the threat of financial ruin.

This is not to mention the use of fears, nearly paranoiac, fears of outside attacks, of foreigners, or of those in our society who mean us harm.

Imposed Change

Since the new society is built to follow the rules of a new ideology, it is clear that changes must occur. These changes emanate not from the needs of the citizenry, but from the requirements of the ideology and the needs of the ruling elite.

Therefore, changes are imposed from the top down...mandated by a master plan. Any resistance to those changes are met with increasing repression and finally with oppression.

Pushback and Increasing Frustration Led to Violence

As the ideological underpinnings of the establishment begin to be exposed as leaving out the ordinary citizenry and the repression increases…as the gloves come off…the levels of frustration begin to grow. People begin to see that there is no sustainable future for them and certainly not for their children.

Now people have a choice to make. Do they simply ignore the realities, either not believing the exposed reality or simply accepting their fate as powerless individuals in the face of overwhelming power, or do they find ways to stand up for themselves?

If they choose disempowered acceptance, they damage not only their links to humanity, but the very possibility of a humanized future. In effect they become collaborators with an oppressive system, complicit in that oppression. Their basic fate is despair.

If they choose to claim some degree of their empowerment as human beings, they have several paths they can follow.

They can work within the system for change. This is proven to not be a very effective approach since the establishment is created to thwart exactly that kind of change, but only slowly and over time so as not to discourage this approach.

They can more overtly resist the agenda of the establishment, trying to slow it down or, occasionally stop it. This is more like working to stop the leaks in the sea wall that was meant to protect a democratic society from the ocean of wealth and power trying to inundate it. The goal of the establishment is to increase the cracks and holes in that sea wall in their attempts to undermine it and eventually declare that it

102

was always untenable and have us give up on it. So, this, too, is working within their purview.

A third way is to give in to the utter frustration of trying to get the establishment to change and to see only violence as a solution. This is the place in which almost any alternative looks better than a continuation of the "same old, same old". Understanding that there is no way to win a direct confrontation with the enormous power of the establishment, they use guerrilla tactics, even self-sacrifice and what many would call terrorism to disrupt an oppressive system.

The fourth way is to change back to the old democratic paradigm that had served this society quite well (but not perfectly) in the past and work to improve on it. This path is based on the knowledge that no system or establishment can continue without, at least, the tacit support of its citizens. As more and more citizens desert the system to support democracy again, the old system will begin to crumble simply from lack of a supporting populace. This provides a positive alternative for the energies of an unhappy populace. It is like leaving a house that has become toxic or has been undermined. One would begin to build a new house in a safe and sustainable environment for their survival and the survival of those they care about. They would even help their neighbors who found themselves in similar situations. This is the most effective and most positive and least violent or frustrating option.

Measures of Decline

If you were to actually chart what has been happening to this nation in the last several decades, it would become abundantly clear the control has shifted away from democracy and control by the citizens of this nation to control by an economic elite concerned with protecting itself and expanding, normalizing, institutionalizing and consolidating its power.

103

Here are some of the items that might be included in such a chart:

• Taxes shift from progressive to regressive
• Weakened environmental standards
• Reduced economic standards and controls
• Cuts to social programs
• Erosion of voter protections
• Declining support for public programs
• Increased privatization of government functions
• Tax revenues redirected to support business and corporate profits
• Regulatory agencies captured by business, finance, and corporations
• Politicization of the court system
• Media and social institutions dominated by the economic elite
• Growth of the military and security state
• Information controlled and censored
• Attacks on whistleblowers and transparency
• Expanded secrecy and civil rights restrictions justified by national security
• Surge in gun ownership and gun deaths
• Demonization of science that challenges elite worldviews
• Criminalization of dissent
• Financial survival tied to high-risk investments
• Push to privatize Social Security and Medicare
• Health care and prisons increasingly privatized for profit
• Retirement programs under attack
• Broken promises of deferred compensation and pension systems
• Disempowerment of labor and stagnant wages/benefits
• Productivity gains no longer linked to wage increases

Saving Democracy-2025

- Rising income inequality
- Endless wars yielding endless corporate war profits
- Military service reduced to high-risk jobs; support roles privatized
- Global increases in regime change, coups, and nation-building for profit
- Expanded projection of U.S. military and financial power
- Warfare privatized and covert: drones, assassinations, secret missions
- Restrictions on voting rights
- Increased violence toward non–white Anglo-Saxon males
- Denial of climate change
- Unwavering support for fossil fuels
- Money dominates elections and national policy
- Declining opportunity for ordinary voices to be heard, silencing creative, capable citizens

The New American Feudalism

Now the economic elite are willing to switch to a new vehicle to continue their dominance. They were willing to shift to the most blatant expression of their dominance, a de facto king (a CEO) and a ruling aristocracy of wealth. All citizens would need to learn that they existed only at the pleasure of the King/CEO. If they tried to thwart him, they would lose favor, and he would use the powerful engines of the government against them to marginalize them or destroy them.

Those who curry his favor would be free to exploit and plunder the nation, i.e., just look at the stock market and the structural and procedural changes that benefit the economic elite.

Some ordinary citizens might find favor with his fickle taste, and some might be entertaining or have enough celebrity to make the cut, but the ordinary citizens are now seen as mere peasants and serfs to be used by the economic elite to be exploited to keep them living in the style to which they had become accustomed.

The citizens are kept in line by the promise of jobs, for which they often seemed to be willing to sell out all principles including their democratic heritage. And, as in Medieval Europe, they are taught to distrust any who were different or who wanted change. And "there be dragons" with the demonizing of other races, women, other lifestyles, foreigners, and outside threats… "terrorists". It has become a time of fear, defensiveness, distrust, superstition and belief that the old ways before logic and science really had the best solutions.

The new American Feudalism, rule from the top down.

All of this within my lifetime! Somehow our leadership has taken us from democracy all the way back to where we were before the American Revolution, to a new kind of feudalism.

106

Warning: They Are Not Finished Yet!!

The economic elite is probably aware of the waning public support for their economic system and their establishment, but they have been preparing for this day for a long time. They knew all along that their system would enrich them at our expense and every day they continued under that pretense gave them one more day to prepare for the inevitable disillusionment.

They have several lines of defense for just this likelihood. First of all, they can continue to encourage people to think that the system can be changed from within. If people can just make enough phone calls to their representatives, those representatives will turn away from their biggest financial backers and do the right thing. If they work hard enough, they can eventually elect good and true people to Congress and then they can pass all those laws that will correct the problems, even though the system is flooded with money, the electoral system has been horribly corrupted, and Congress continues to do the bidding of the economic elite in spite of all their head-shaking and hand-wringing. If they work on one issue long enough and hard enough with enough people, the system will have to see the light and change.

That is an approach prepared as a huge energy sink for the passion, energy and resources of a public that wants to believe there is still a way within the system to create the kind of change that is necessary to right the ship of Democracy.

A second way is to use propaganda and intimidation to discourage people from pursuing major systemic change.

A third way, if need be, is to put the huge, secretive and powerful security agencies to work on any who have the timidity to challenge their power. Remember the security system is a system that is accountable to no external powers, being only internally accountable within the systems themselves. This is an apparatus which has the legal power to silence anyone about whatever it chooses with the threat of basically disappearing those who cause too much trouble.

They eat whistleblowers for lunch and have destroyed many who have let people know what is being done in our name and with our tax money. Their powers make the fatwa against Salman Rushdie that drove him into hiding for several years look trivial.

The administrative head of that establishment is still intact serving the economic elite with full funding and walls still intact, manned by the police and the military, and by the best security system ever created.

Popular support, even though much of it might have been tacit support, provided the mortar to hold up the temples and, to some degree, the wall. With that support waning they are willing to use blood and fear as replacements for that mortar.

Last Gasp/Imposed Power

Once you have given notice to the powers-that-be that you have seen through their devices and therefore their influence is waning, they begin to marshal their defenses. They want to make it clear that just because you see through their games, they can still remain in control simply by using the power of their establishment.

That power can be used to intimidate, to manipulate and to impose solutions simply by using the levers of power they still retain. They are entrenched and it will be difficult to dislodge them.

But Wait...

It may appear as though there is no way to take that structure down anymore, but that is not true. No system can endure when the people turn away and will no longer support that system, no matter how much blood and fear is used to try to prop it up.

This cannot be an individual fight, but it can only occur when the populace becomes empowered individually once again and will put aside all differences to unify their efforts toward one goal.

Luckily, we already have an acceptable goal...Democracy. It is tried and true and we can walk back to it and reconstruct an establishment that serves all the people and not just a small elite.

They are working hard to prevent us from realizing that truth, but the cat is out of the bag.

Perspective: The Spell of Dependency

Once you have given over control to others or to some kind of mechanism that you have been told will guide your decision-making and absolve you of any responsibility for your own future, or for anyone else's, it is often a difficult journey back to independence and the kind of maturity a sustainable democracy requires of its citizens.

That dependency is a kind of spell that can be comforting but ultimately turns you into a mere resource to be exploited for someone else's ends, no matter how much they might assure you that they are looking out for your welfare. It is disempowering and

Saving Democracy-2025

dehumanizing, turning you into something to be manipulated.

The feel-good moments are not worth the price you pay and will eventually make you willing to do things you would otherwise not consider. You begin to crave a continuation of the spell of dependency because you can no longer see yourself as strong enough to deal with life without that spell.

It is like an addiction and breaking that addiction, that habit requires you to break the spell of dependency and create a new spell of independence and empowerment-i.e., you are capable of making your own decisions in your life. In fact, you are the only one who can make those decisions to keep yourself healthy as a human being.

In the process you begin to understand how dehumanizing the entire process of dependency has been, and would continue to be, if you stayed under its spell.

Time to Choose Our Future: Two Visions

We are in the midst of one of those watershed moments for this nation. It is time to choose to stay the course with an alien economic system that has not worked for the ordinary citizens and has seriously damaged our democracy, or to switch tracks and move back toward democracy and citizen participation for a sustainable human future.

It is a choice of an authoritarian future rule by an economic elite or a democratic future, which is our real heritage.

It is important to remember that top-down change is engineered change that is an attempt to make human reality fit some theory, agenda or worldview of some
elite. Nature usually steps in to show the life follows its own patterns and not the patterns of any elite in spite of how confident they are of their superiority.

To change requires risk and courage and a renewal of the indomitable American Spirit which will release the incredible resiliency, energy and creativity that America has been known for. It is hard to doubt that, given the option, the citizenry of this nation will once again choose a participatory democracy as their future.

Why Vision is Important

Vision, as one might guess, is crucial to finding our way through the problems of today and to having a plan to navigate the future. Without vision, one might as well be blind and simply go stumbling and groping haphazardly through life.

We are always following someone's vision, whether it is enunciated clearly or not, and we need to understand what that vision might be, what the destination might be, what role we are to play, and whether or not we want to be a part of that voyage.

It is a watershed time in which we must choose the vision for our future, the future of our loved ones, our fellow-citizens and the future of this nation, the world, and, perhaps, the human race.

The Dystopian Vision: Passive Acceptance

This is the vision of the American future that the ruling elite, the 1%, the Rich & Powerful have in store for us. It is a society run by absentee landlords who treat us like a colony to be used and plundered for profit with its people seen simply as economic units to be exploited until they no longer offer any economic value and then to be discarded as useless. After the resources and people have been used up, they simply leave the mess behind and move on to other locations that offer a better return on investment.

They operate like organized crime, ruthlessly destroying whatever stands in their way. They impose a kind of police state and their own sets of rules and laws, they control the means of communication, the social institutions and all of the instruments of governance so they can intimidate any dissent and quash any attempt at an uprising. It is a perfectly predictable and controlled society that can provide maximum profits and almost no resistance.

Those who manage such systems receive the highest pay and bonuses, not just from profits, but also for keeping the system running smoothly and the workers under control.

It is a vision of totally privatized public functions in which our taxes simply provide profit streams for private corporations, and we no longer have any real voice in those public functions.

It is a vision of a leadership so addicted to the accumulation of wealth and power that they will use anything available to feed that habit, no matter how destructive it might be.

It is a vision with gigantic corporations controlling the lives of people and the Rich & Powerful protecting them and feeding off them.

It is a vision of a society walled-in and propagandized…a kind of Oz…where we are only allowed to hear what serves their purposes and we are issued specially tinted green glasses, so we see it all in a positive economic light.

It is a vision where certain ideas are off-limits, almost like the orthodoxy of a religion where certain ideas are blasphemy or heretical. A few that come to mind now are any questions about the validity of unfettered free-market capitalism to solve all human problems, questioning the wisdom of the rich, questioning what those countries we financially and economically support are doing or questioning the military or security service, or even secrecy or surveillance or secret warfare.

To choose this vision, you must be willing to accept the dominance of an alien ideology that has come to occupy this nation with its collaborators and its acolytes of greed in the new religion of greed. It is to choose a heartless and soulless ideology that is willing to destroy life and natural beauty in its obsessive drive for more wealth. It is to choose an economically engineered society dominated by corporations which-with their masters who manipulate the markets-determine priorities with ruthless efficiency, where life, sustainability and the human spirit are of low, or no, priority.

Perspective: The Dystopian Express

The Dystopian Express is a state-of-the-art train. It is shiny and new and offers all the amenities to make it very desirable to board. However, it isn't really about the engine and the cars, or the amenities, it is about the direction that it is heading.

It is taking its passengers into the land ruled by the economic elite. It is going further inland on their tectonic plate and away from the democratic tectonic plate. The land the train passes through is scoured of life-a wasteland, played out with mining, oil extraction and logging. It is a land full of disruptions, earthquakes, and volcanoes, bursting economic bubbles making life and work much riskier.

Think of the established system as having laid the tracks toward the future they want to secure for themselves. Once that is done, it does not matter who the engineer is, or who the crew is, the train will continue following the tracks toward the predetermined goal.

We, the passengers riding on the train, assume that the chosen direction will deliver us to a destination in which we can live prosperous, safe and secure lives.

If we realize that the train is going in a direction that will not really benefit us, and instead, will be only beneficial to those in charge of the train, we might wish to change things.

We are told we can vote to change the engineer and/ or the crew and those who supply support services. We do change the role players occasionally, sometimes in the

114

desire to change direction and sometimes to slow down or speed up the journey to the predetermined destination.

We begin to realize that the train may temporarily slow down or speed up, but it will never stop or back up, let alone change direction. The tracks have been laid and there is only one direction this train can ever go. Changing the cast of characters never results in any change of direction. It has all been foreordained by the ruling establishment.

Meanwhile we are told that we should not leave the train if we hope to survive. Instead, we are strongly encouraged, and at times intimidated, to stay the course, whether or not we like it. We are told to trust them, that the rewards will come later.

We may even begin to realize that we are little more than unwilling participants, but are told that others, wiser than we, will make those decisions for us. We are left to only have faith in their good intentions and ignore any realities that might make us question that.

We may have noticed, while passing through the relatively unspoiled landscapes, that even those are in the process of burning, being blown away, or flooded, that there is a fence alongside the tracks on the left side that is hiding something from our view, and we wonder what that is.

But it is far easier to simply stop looking out the windows and watch the screens that offer great entertainment. Besides that, the food is good, and the drinks keep coming. Not a bad life on this train-if you don't pay attention to where it is taking you.

115

The Democratic Vision: Empowered Alternative

The democratic vision is a vision of mature and empowered citizens who value inclusiveness, connections, relationships and community, fairness, and equality; who value life and the human spirit; who refuse to be dominated and will work to safeguard their right to self-determination above all else

The democratic vision begins with the ordinary citizens being at the heart of governance, decision-making and oversight.

It is a humanizing vision.

It is a vision that only requires clear sight and open information for an informed citizenry to make decisions and solve real problems.

It is a vision that reestablishes participation and involvement in community, state and national governance.

It is a vision that was alive and well in this country, so it seems relatively normal.

It is a vision of equality and social justice.

It is a vision of equal opportunity and a level playing field once again.

It is a vision where wealth does not determine what happens socially or politically.

It is a vision of universal voting where all citizens are encouraged and supported in their desire to vote.

It is a vision in which education and health care are rights of citizenship.

It is a vision that values all citizens and provide social safety nets and help for those in need, as we would for those in our family.

116

It is a vision in which the only entitlement would be those that go with the title of "Citizen" and not those of wealth or class.

It is a vision in which profits are put in perspective again and human betterment is no longer seen simply as an economic opportunity for some corporation.

It is a vision in which military and security decisions are made in an open and democratic arena.

It is a vision of a foreign policy that reflects the positive human values of the nation.

It is a vision in which work is valued, and jobs pay a livable wage, and that advancement and retirement are there to support the dignity of citizenship and hard work.

Perspective: *The Democracy Local*

There is an alternative to the bright and shiny Dystopian Express, but it is pulled by a hard-working, well-used, dependable engine that has been around for a while.

It is not an express, but instead a local, stopping at every town to pick up those who have lost faith in the neoliberal economic model and are now interested in going back to a democracy again to build a Democratic future.

There is a fare to be paid, but your willingness to be involved in keeping the engine working and the train maintained-your willingness to pitch in with your energy and your resources is all that is required. That and a willingness to be inclusive and cooperative, building a community that can work together to face whatever challenges come along.

117

People now have the opportunity to decide to transfer to this older working train of Democracy that is leaving for the tectonic plate that offers sustainable life, support for the human spirit and human values, where life is once again treasured, and Democracy can once again thrive.

It is already clear that large and small train cars are forming and filling up with those who are working for that new future and are now ready to join that train to show the social momentum of that paradigm shift that is growing every day.

As we watch, we see people coming from everywhere in our society to couple their cars and their hopes to this train that is moving toward a real future of participatory democracy. It is an opportunity for all citizens to find their empowered American Spirit once again and bloom into an inclusive and thriving human society.

It is a challenge to our human spirit, our courage, to shake off the easy complacency of letting others decide our life and future as well as that of our children and even the entire world.

118

Failure of Past Attempts at Change Within the System

Over the last several decades there have been several attempts to stop the destructiveness of turning our nation over to an economic aristocracy.

After the fiasco of Nixon and his attempts to manipulate elections and then the pardon granted by Ford, the people voted for a respite for a short time with Carter.

The power of the economic aristocracy reasserted itself with the elections of Reagan and then Bush, in the process garnering more power and dominance.

The democratizing voices of the people reasserted themselves with the election of Clinton who, after years of attack by that elite, was eventually co-opted by the ruling elite.

Then we had the disaster of the second Bush giving top-heavy tax cuts to the rich, declaring open season on the finances of the nation as well as attacks on democracy after 9/11, and finally allowing that financial elite to run the economy off the tracks, in 2008.

Obama was elected by an outpouring of desire to go back to democracy and to control the economic elite to stop the disaster. The people were hoping for an FDR moment again.

But he was somehow co-opted by the time he was elected, and we watched as he turned the economic decisions over to Wall Street insiders and we watched as many of the Bush policies continued, and income inequality continued to grow as we bailed out the rich and pushed the ordinary Americans under the bus.

And finally, we had Bernie Sanders, who actually told us how things really are and how we could get back to a sane democracy. The people responded whole-heartedly and overwhelmingly to this message and Bernie looked to be on the verge of being swept into power. But the economic

119

aristocracy was too strong to allow that threat, and they used the Hilary Clinton campaign and the Democratic National Committee to destroy Bernie's campaign and to assure the continuation of rule by that economic elite.

An Existential Crisis

We must remember to put this situation in the context of the earlier tests of democracy within this nation. This is another such test.

This is the perfect storm: democracy being replaced by rule by an economic elite; technology and weaponry perfecting a security system any authoritarian ruler would die for; human life and the environment being monetized and destroyed to fuel ever-growing profits; with the focus shifting to financial and economic issues while dehumanizing the society; and finally, nature is telling us, in no uncertain terms, that our environmental abuses have caused so much destruction that human life, and life for much of nature, will be unsustainable without drastic human action.

Meanwhile those with the power, merely slough it off, sure, in their hubris, that they can either buy a solution, or pay off the offenders, or certainly just negotiate better terms and find a way to make a profit…perhaps even a killing in the market with such a crisis.

If you have any hope for your survival, the survival of those you care for, our society, life and our planet, there is no option but to act to replace this powerful and destructive system.

No one can afford to simply wait it out as a spectator.

The ruling system is only responsive to one thing and that is power.

The real power we have is our overwhelming numbers.

We must be totally unified behind the idea of Democracy to replace this destructive system. Only then will we be able to confront the real issues and begin to save ourselves and our planet.

This is similar to France after WWII getting rid of the Vichy Government which had ruled during the German occupation of France or Gandhi getting rid of England as a colonial power in India. There is a need to totally replace the corrupt government and its laws and replace them by going back to democracy.

Perspective: The Choice: Two Trains-All Aboard!

This last election (2016) signaled the end to any illusions that neoliberal economics was going to work for us or that the leadership of the economic aristocracy cared about what we thought, except to try to exploit us and find ways to exploit us even more.

With those illusions being shattered by the earthquake of that election, we are faced with a stark new reality, but also with a window of opportunity to choose a different direction for our future.

Because of the exposed weaknesses and failures of the present establishment, this is a moment of choice. It is not a choice which will remain open. The window of opportunity is wide open but will begin to quickly close as time elapses and the new reality is normalized. It is a choice of which paradigm we choose for our future.

It is about survival and courage in measures we have not needed in recent history. We have faced adversity

121

before, but never has it been so clearly an existential choice. In recent history we have been involved in wars, but they directly affected only a part of the population and were all on foreign soil. We have had some terrorism, both domestic and foreign, but again they only directly affected a small portion of our citizenry.

This election was a domestic event which affected the entire population and requires us to rethink our future and our options. It cannot be avoided. Either we submissively continue to give our tacit consent to the exploitation of our world for the profits of the few, or we change direction and move back to a democratic and sustainable direction and future.

One way to get some perspective on the moment is to think about the choice to be made as a choice of which train to board.

Think of the established system as having laid the tracks toward the future they want to secure for themselves. Once that is done, it does not matter who the engineer is, or who the crew is, the train will continue following the tracks toward that predetermined goal.

The train that the economic elite hopes will carry us to that future is the Dystopian Express. We are familiar with it because, without realizing it, we have been on-board that train for the last several decades. It is the train that took us to this land of earthquakes and destruction and is fueled by the neoliberal economic system.

Lately, as we were on the Dystopian Express, we began to notice that, outside our windows, there is another set of tracks being quietly built. At first, we think it is just to transport more people to the destination more efficiently, but then we hear that it is a set of tracks being built by those who want to change direction, not just the engineer and supporting cast, but the entire system of the Dystopian Railway with its predetermined destination.

We also learned that some of those tracks already existed and were apparently abandoned and fenced off when the new establishment decided to build new tracks in the opposite direction. Those old tracks were from our past when a different system had established a more democratic direction for the society.

And, recently, looking out the windows, we begin to see some passenger cars full of people like ourselves on the other tracks. We find, through the underground, that there are those who will help us transfer safely if we wish to take the other train. We begin to recognize some of the passenger cars from our train on the other track with people we know. They apparently have uncoupled cars from the end of the Dystopian Express and moved over to the other tracks.

We also hear that additional engines are being built to take that train in the new direction…a direction with a much more promising destination for ordinary folks like us.

Some still hope that they can simply change engineers or change the crew, and everything will come out right somehow. But as time goes by it becomes harder and harder to sustain that illusion and their numbers begin to dwindle.

It has become clear to almost everyone that simply electing others to fill the roles in this established system does not change the direction one iota and that the only hope is to leave that system and begin to build an establishment to take us in the direction of a democracy and a sustainable world once again.

The result of this political earthquake of an election, is like we are all in the train station and must choose to continue on the same train, the Dystopian Express, that took us into this wasteland and into this last election, or we decide to transfer to the older working train, the Democratic Local, that is on the journey back to Democracy and a sustainable life, supporting the human spirit and human values, where life is once again treasured and Democracy can once again thrive.

One train is the modern and shiny Dystopian Express with all its glitter,-its bells and whistles-which will take us to those empty promises of a dystopian future. The other train is the Democratic Local, a working train, not so shiny but very dependable, which will stop to pick up any who want to board and are willing to work for their fares. It is already clear that there are large cars and small cars full of people who have been working on democratizing issues, people who have been trying to change the direction of the Dystopian Express but now see that they will never succeed and are now ready to couple their cars to the growing length of the Democratic Local.

Saving Democracy-2025

They now understand that we need to have a nation with a democracy, not one ruled by a small economic aristocracy. Without democratic decision-making in place, progress on these issues is all but impossible.

Those organizations, and many other small groups - even individuals-are now ready to connect their hopes and support to that train to show the united social momentum of the paradigm shift back to democracy that is growing every day.

It is a challenge to our human spirit, our courage to shake off the easy complacency of letting others decide our life and future as well as that of our children and even the entire world.

It is an "All Aboard" moment. Once the trains begin to move it will be too late. Our fate will be sealed.

The Final Trick: Dump Trump

Although the economic elite was OK with Donald Trump winning the election since he came out of the economic elite, they were not particularly happy with his "loose cannon" approach to governance. They still managed to survive quite well...thank you very much...as evidenced by the meteoric gains of the stock market...their real measure of success.

But the growing fears and frustrations of the nation with the antics of his ego-centric methods of governance create questions of his sustainability.

Never fear, the economic elite are ever flexible, so they are busy laying the groundwork for a transition back to the moderate guidance of more recent presidencies who willingly did the bidding of those economic elites to retain their support and stay in power.

This is when we need to understand that changing the engineers on the train does not alter the direction the tracks are taking us. We have seen the destination, and it does not bode well for us.

Those tracks have been laid by the economic elite and improved upon by neoliberal economics. The economic elite is fine with us changing engineers as long as the train stays on the tracks they have laid for us.

Their hope is that, after Trump, the smiling and moderate faces of the establishment candidates will look good to us and we will willingly continue the trip on those tracks, even accepting the negative results and trajectories that existed before Trump because they look better by comparison.

That would be an "out of the frying pan, into the fire" kind of solution.

It is important to warn others of this ploy and the short-sightedness of going back to the "same-old, same-old" as some sort of quick fix. Being willing to go back to the "old normal"

126

is just another way of putting off the real solutions and watching the window of opportunity slam in our face once again.

If the economic elite can pull this off, they will be busy reconstituting moderate (meaning establishment approved) political parties; the Democratic Party, purged of the progressives, and the Republican Party tamping down the worst of the Tea Party radicals.

All of this while glossing over the real needs for a more democratic society. Talk about putting lipstick on the pig while also dressing it up with a suit and tie, giving it a big smile and a soothing voice.

All of the facades that came down in the earthquake will be rebuilt as will the walls of the illusion of the American Oz and we will be issued new glasses, still with green lenses.

The Dystopian Express will be refurbished, making it even more tempting than before, and people will again begin to line up to board.

Meanwhile the Democracy Train will sit idly at the depot while they prepare it for the junkyard once again.

How to Reclaim Democracy: A Plan for Action

Introduction

So, as the political earthquake has shattered the façade of neoliberal economics and after we realized that we have been seduced into believing its benevolent promises, we are faced with the reality of what remains. What remains is a weakened and faltering paradigm, which is deeply entrenched and in control of very powerful propaganda tools, as well as incredible military and economic power. This is not even to mention the very effective apparatus of a technologically advanced security state.

Our challenge is three-fold; first we must recover from being victimized by the illusory promises of economic security, but we must find a way to not only survive the entrenched system, but also, to find a way out from under the occupation and rebuild the structure needed for our return to democracy.

Secondly, we must walk away from the neoliberal economic system, withdrawing our support.

Third, we must find ways to, not only unify, but to keep that unity in-tact.

The goal is a unified, balanced, inclusive, sustainable, humanized democracy.

Our major tools are numbers…a vast majority of humankind…our resilience, our empowered might and our creativity.

Although one of our first reactions might be anger at those who perpetuated the hoax, that energy might be better used in strategic ways to begin to restructure our democratic heritage, rather than to simply fight and oppose them or try to get even or get them to acknowledge their errors.

128

The other reality is that their entrenched establishment has been built to be impenetrable and not likely to be defeated by a frontal attack, or even by trying to change the system from within. We can ultimately weaken and finally let it fall of its own weight by simply beginning to withdraw our tacit support. No system can continue without the support of those which it serves if they withdraw.

Working within that system to affect change is like pouring your energy and resources into a series of great energy sinkholes. Instead, it is by far more productive to find a positive alternative to support. One in which our energy is appreciated and whose outcomes take us where we want to go.

That alternative is Democracy.

The Wisdom of Perspective

So, from this new perspective we have learned that those who had accumulated wealth and power were, from the very beginning of this nation, continually trying to devise ways to usurp the power of this nation by building a government guided by that economic elite. At the same time, other forces have been moving toward a more democratic nation.

Putting our history in perspective, we have had other watershed moments in this nation: first with the Revolutionary War, then the Civil War and then the Crash of 1929. Each of those watershed moments required a choice between allowing an economic elite to rule or to choose democracy again.

These two forces were in constant conflict over whether government was to sustain that wealth and power or whether it was to help all its citizens move toward a sustainable future through a more inclusive democracy.

While the wealth was in power there continued to be boom and bust economic crises-1929 and 2008 being the most notable. During periods of more democratic oversight, like the

Saving Democracy-2025

New Deal, the needs of the ordinary citizens were addressed, and safeguards were put in place to protect against exploitation.

Since then, the rich and powerful have been working quietly to not only limit the democratic urges of the nation, but finally to dismantle them. They found a number of vehicles for their use. There was the anti-Communism, most apparent in the 1950s but still continuing as an undercurrent. There was the Cold War. There was the space race. There were democratizing attempts in Central and South America, all of which were labeled as Communist and defeated.

And then there was terrorism and what was labeled the threat of radical Islam.

The nation's focus was on spending money on the military, the security systems and weapons development.

While all of this was going on the rich and powerful found the tool of neoliberal economics, with conservatives leading the way, and with the pseudo intellectual justification for market morality.

By now there had been blatant attempts to make this nation a one-party system under Nixon. There was endless corruption and flouting of rules under Reagan and Bush. There was the destruction of unionism and eventually the middle class. There was opening up the floodgates of money in politics first with the Bush II tax give-away to the rich and finally the Supreme Court decision of Citizens United.

And then there was the attack on voting with questionable voting machine technology, purging voting rolls, gerrymandering and finally outright voter suppression.

The citizens of the nation sat still for all of this while under the spell of the empty promises of neoliberal economics. They had been seduced by the illusions presented and maintained by the ideology and had become addicted to the need to hope for a good outcome in the face of dwindling economic benefits in their own realities.

Finally, the illusion could no longer be sustained. The tectonic pressures were building. Reality had made that illusion and the establishment that had been built to support and sustain it, irrelevant. The representatives of that system could not muster the support to be reelected, especially when a real representative of the will of the people was so rudely pushed out.

And so, the 2016 election of Donald Trump was the final working out of that change the establishment had worked so long and hard to prevent. It was a step too far and the earthquake occurred bringing down the walls of the American Oz.

The establishment crumbled before our eyes and the illusions were exposed as reality swept in. The real power and purpose of the illusion was clear for all to see.

The final act of that establishment was to put forward a totally unqualified pretender who would sustain that establishment with all its tools and at any cost.

Very few could doubt the need for change, for a new paradigm. Fortunately, we already had a handy and workable paradigm from our past, Democracy.

But people were in shock trying to make sense out of what just happened. They began to realize that they had been conned out of their democracy and their resources. They were angry and were ready to lash out against a bad system.

However, the only workable solution was to move back to a democratic system…to be for something positive and not just against something that had hurt them.

To do this, first they had to recover from the spell of neoliberal economics and find ways to reclaim their maturity

131

and empowerment so they could stand up and unify in their support of such a change.

They needed to develop, or rediscover, effective means of creating such a change, understanding the power of an enraged economic elite and an establishment, weakened, but still standing, with multiple resources.

The Dominant Worldview

The worldview that has been dominant, certainly for the last several decades in this nation, is that of unfettered free-market capitalism, neoliberal economics, as the engine that will lead us to fulfilling the human dreams and producing a sustainable world.

As with any paradigm, it remains acceptable as long as it continues to work. Often, as the paradigm begins to show weakness and seems not to be working as promised, the establishment that has grown up around the paradigm, begins to provide explanations for those weaknesses and failures, to explain them away as aberrations and assure us that staying the course will eventually prove the veracity of the entire venture.

As the dichotomy between observed reality and those explanations grows larger, more and more time and energy are poured into retaining the illusion of success, eventually leading to a need to control information and at times intimidate the people to continue to support the failing paradigm.

At some point the illusion can no longer be sustained and when the illusion falls away, the failing system is exposed with all its flaws, clearly no longer viable, but still attempting to continue through force and intimidation…the raw use of power and wealth to sustain a dead paradigm.

The curtain has fallen, revealing the Great Oz to be a group of old men sitting around a table in the midst of technology used to create the illusion of wisdom and power.

132

Here in the US, we have just gone through a seismic shift, tearing away the illusions of the unsustainable paradigm of free-market capitalism as the engine that was to take us to paradise. The paradigm of neoliberal economics clearly no longer works. It has led us to a world run by oligarchs and autocrats who are all related by similar ideologies in the same way that all the European monarchs were related by the paradigm of monarchy in the 19th and early 20th Centuries.

That paradigm has brought us back to a world run by wealth and power with a powerful aristocracy. Meanwhile, the ordinary people have once again, become subjects, exploited to finance the lifestyles, as well as the games and adventures of that ruling class. And the planet itself is there to provide resources for their use without regard to consequences.

Recovering from the disillusionment of being conned by those who posed as our leaders who appeared to be caring about our welfare, requires quite a shift and a need to understand how not to get caught in the net of victimhood.

Perspective: The Divorce

A ruling political paradigm is a social contract between those who developed that paradigm and the society which accepts the legitimacy of that paradigm. When that paradigm is exposed as simply a ploy to extort the wealth and resources of that society, it is like a marriage in which one spouse finds out that the other was just using them. Instead of truly caring for them, the real purpose all along was to transfer the resources of that relationship into the other spouse's individual account and then to walk away.

133

Talk about betrayal and deceit! There is the embarrassment of being played, of being naive enough to be taken like that. There is frustration and anger. There is rage and a desire for vengeance and punishment.

Unfortunately, the other party simply turns its back on us and walks away without looking back or even responding to us.

In the case of the failed promises of the neoliberal economic system as with any disillusionment over a failed relationship, there is a feeling of betrayal and an urge for anger and revenge. This, however, just keeps us stuck in a kind of victimhood, trying to change the dynamics of what has already happened or to get some kind of satisfaction in punishing those who we feel wronged us.

The key to breaking the spell of victimhood is to claim our own empowerment and to create a new and productive, more positive, spell for ourselves.

However, what we really need is a focus on moving on in a healthier and more productive way. There is a saying that the best revenge is to live well. We need to turn our backs on the broken and inadequate system and move back to our roots, our sustainable democratic heritage.

Recovery

Introduction

Recovery is a process of letting go of the old with its stability and predictability, even when it was based on our disempowerment. It is a time to rediscover our mature and empowered self to step toward a new life. It is about finding the common groundedness of life to create a new stability from which to move into a new future.

Perspective: Snap Out of It

There are times when we need a wake-up call to connect to reality. We have all had times in our lives when we have operated in a world of our own, disconnected from the realities of life. We have all found that we cannot sustain those worlds and continue to exist as humans in the structures of the realities of life.

This is a cautionary tale taken from a real-life experience during our move from California to our retirement home in North Central Minnesota.

My wife and I had a refrigerator magnet that had a young girl reprimanding a younger sibling by sternly saying, "Snap out of it," something we all probably heard during our childhood to get us back to reality.

We had found a perfect place near the Mississippi River, quiet with a small woods on one side, an island in the river and not much development on the other side of the river.

During our first early spring my wife and I were clearing some brush by the river. I was about 20 yards away from her and there were fish jumping in the river. While I worked, I heard a splash and looked up thinking it was another fish. I was going to tell my wife but, when I looked, I couldn't find her.

We had been working on a fairly steep part of the yard right by the river and she apparently had lost her balance and hit her head on a tree on her way into the river, although I did not know it at the time.

Then I saw she was in the river peacefully doing her dog-paddle and seemingly unconcerned.

The water was cold, and hypothermia was a concern, and the cut bank made it impossible to climb out, so I didn't want to go in and find that we were both stuck there. There were no other people around...we were on our own.

I found something to reach out to her to bring her to the cut bank of the river so she could hold onto some roots while I devised a way to get her out.

As I was telling her to grab what I was offering, she seemed unconcerned and continued to dog-paddle blithely down the river. I finally got her attention and did get her to the bank willing to hold on to some roots till I got back with some way to extricate her. She was still quite unconcerned.

Finally, I said to her, now that you are near the bank just try to put your feet down. That took some convincing, but she finally did and found that the water was just chest high.

As it turned out, a crew we had hired to do some landscape work just happened to arrive at that moment with two young men who were able to lift her from the river.

As I walked her to the house and got her out of her wet clothes and into something dry, it became clear that she was suffering from a concussion. Despite her complaints I took her to the hospital, and she ended up staying overnight and came home soon, fairly unscathed by the experience.

The reason it is a cautionary tale is that it exemplifies what happens when your worldview is disconnected from the realities of the situation. There were at least four pieces of reality that she was oblivious to in her concussed state. First of all was the threat of hypothermia. Second was the fact that I was not in a position to go into the water to help without creating another problem for both of us. Third was the fact that the current in the river would eventually sweep her downriver and over a dam. Lastly, there was no one else near to call for help. (Help did serendipitously appear, thank goodness)

I was her connection to the reality of the rest of the world, and I had a hard time persuading her to pay attention.

The final piece was that she began to reconnect with reality when she stopped swimming and found that there was, indeed, solid ground under her feet offering her *stability. It was a place from which she could begin her journey back to reality.*

The moral of the story is that when we are in an artificial and illusory reality, we need to heed those voices who are there to help us reconnect with a more grounded and solid reality from which our transition can begin.

Breaking the Spell of Neoliberal Economics

Breaking the spell of neoliberal economics is simply the process of understanding that we are in control of our own lives, our own destinies, and that the spell was self-inflicted. It is understandable that we were seduced by the siren songs of neoliberal economics with its promises of a secure financial future. But we now see that it was a ruse.

We need to walk away from it, like a bad marriage or relationship, and not waste time trying to change it, assess blame or try to get even. We must direct our energy into a productive future rather than into anger, blame and vengeance which will only keep us connected to that older, destructive spell.

We must choose the freedom of our newfound empowerment and go on to create a powerful and effective spell for ourselves to build a positive and sustainable future for us and for our society.

This takes courage, humility and acceptance of adult responsibility.

Creating the Spell of Democracy

Creating the spell of democracy mostly requires the citizenry to rekindle the American Spirit, reclaim their own empowerment as a free people and invest their time and energy

138

in reconstructing democracy in America. That spell will provide the creative energy to, once again, build a free society to be a beacon for the peoples of the world to emulate. It will free the basic goodness and compassion of the people of this great nation, and we will be glad to support a government that acts in our name for positive actions in our nation and around the world.

Refocusing

Refocusing is difficult. If you have been hurt, or deceived, or exploited, the tendency it to be angry and want to punish those who hurt you, or to get vengeance...to get your pound of flesh in payment for the suffering you endured.

That may feel rewarding in the short run, but it keeps you tied to those who caused the problems and keeps you playing in their arena, in some ways, by their rules. It keeps you locked within the existing system.

One of the sayings to get past this is, "The best revenge is to live well". You need to break free and focus on a healthier system to restore your balance and become truly empowered once again. If you walk away from their system, they lose their power over you.

It requires courage and an adult response to problems.

Avoiding Distractions

One of the last-ditch efforts of the dying structure of neoliberal economics is to distract us by focusing on attention getting stories of scandal, mayhem and fear, to prevent us from focusing on the problems that the system has created. We focus on the destruction of hurricanes and wild-fires but do not begin to address the underlying problems of man-made environmental changes...in fact we seem to be doubling down on coal and gas production. We focus on the pain inflicted in

Saving Democracy-2025

the Las Vegas mass killings but refuse to deal with meaningful gun control. We are still arguing over the results of the last presidential elections, so we don't have to deal with the major flaws in this economic system that is destroying us.

The economic elite, who are doing just fine under Trump, want us to keep thinking that if we had chosen Hillary Clinton as president, we would not still be on the same tracks, going in the same direction on the same Dystopian Express to oblivion.

The discussions should be about the issues that Bernie Sanders brought to light and not about who we should have chosen as the fateful engineer on the Dystopian Express.

That economic elite is well-practiced and very adept at manipulating public opinion, having learned with years of advertising expertise and media manipulation.

After living for years in the propaganda soup of neoliberal economics, it is hard not to be tempted by the siren call of the latest sensational items.

United We Stand

"United we stand, divided we fall".

"A house divided against itself, cannot stand".

Here is the really important and practical message: In order to effectively counter the power of the establishment that has grown up around neoliberal economics and the economic aristocracy that controls it, we must become single-minded and totally unified.

We have spent years wandering in the wilderness, perplexed by our inability to influence the direction of that establishment. We ask ourselves, why can't the 99% simply outnumber, and finally dominate, the 1% who are making all the rules. The answer is simple math. If you have the 99% going in 99 directions, they never really pose a real threat; they are too scattered to mount an effective threat.

Saving Democracy-2025

The error is that we have been encouraged to focus on issues and not on system change. The reality is that nearly all of the issues we care about won't be resolved under the current system, or they will be incredibly hard to resolve.

How has this happened? We have had a huge number of people who have identified the problems that need our attention. We can all probably identify people, books, magazines and documentaries that have done that.

They even have told us what to do to work on making those changes. Nearly always the advice is about working within the system by the rules of the establishment, which is built to thwart us at every turn. It is like being in an abusive relationship and thinking you will be able to change the abuser if you stay. Almost always the only way to break the cycle is to leave and not look back.

The next question is, how do we find something we can all agree on which is so central to our society that it would either make most of the problems moot points or would provide a way to actually resolve those problems in a timely and effective way?

The answer is so obvious and available that we almost overlook it. It is at the heart of everything the American Dream is about and is the very heritage of this nation. It is Democracy itself.

I can't think of any issue or problem that would not disappear or be available to real solutions if we lived in a democracy again. We need to rise above the particular issues of money in politics, or injustice, or income inequality, or environmental degradation and global warming, or injustices, to the next level which encompasses all of those issues and many more.

Who would not be willing to live in a democracy once again?

141

Democracy First

The ultimate way out of our dilemma is to get off the illusory merry-go-round of the neoliberal economic model, get back to the solid ground of reality, break that dizzying spell that has controlled our future and begin the journey back to a balanced, inclusive, sustainable democracy.

The idea is that if we reconstruct our democracy, all of the problems will be seen from a different perspective and solutions will be self-evident, clearly within the DNA of a democratic society, i.e., income inequality, true justice, universal health care, and equal access to education. Other problems will be open to solution when everyone participates in the discussions of democratic solutions, and the discussion is not between an economic elite and the rest of society.

We do not need to reconstruct a new system but only go back to the basic structure of what our democracy was. There will definitely be changes, but the basic concepts and structures already exist and only require the citizens to breathe life back into them and use them to continue the work of forming a more perfect union.

Solutions

Introduction

The idea is to provide ways for ordinary citizens, with all their strengths, talents, creativity, and gifts, to begin to work cooperatively in a variety of ways to change the disastrous direction that unfettered, free-market capitalism is taking this country…to remind them of their overwhelming numbers (99 to 1) and of the powerlessness of the 1% without our work and our support to move them toward their goals.

What is necessary is a means to unify that 99% into a clear movement back to a sustainable model and democratic heritage and away from the current dominance of a system run by an economic aristocracy (the 1%).

The key is to have a unifying focus…a common banner…under which we can all join in that journey…and that banner is Democracy. There are no problems that we face that will not either be solved by a return to Democracy, or that cannot be reasonably resolved by a return to Democracy. So, no one has to stop their work to right the wrongs, or change the direction of this nation, they only have to hitch their train car to the much larger procession of others moving relentlessly toward Democracy. The world will not be able to ignore the sheer length of that train as all the people and organizations couple on to demonstrate the overwhelming strength and support the ideas of Democracy hold for a free people.

The hope is that this will provide a means, by word of mouth, by Facebook and Twitter and other social media, by citizen action, by art, by song, by creative means to help people to once again become actively involved in their future…a sustainable and democratic future.

It will hopefully provide ways to record and document that growing tide for all to see and to help generate momentum

143

and maintain energy and inspiration for a truly important, "Big-Tent" platform for a Citizen's Movement…the train back to Democracy.

The goal is simple, and it needs no formal documents to accomplish its end. It only needs the simple principles of democracy to guide it and the work of the citizens of this nation to inclusively join the process.

Elements

We must understand we are at a major watershed in U.S. history—another chance to choose democracy overrule by an economic aristocracy.

Like any trauma, this moment calls us to dig deep into our national character, finding our empowered democratic selves as a source of courage to reclaim democracy.

It's time to unleash the determination of an engaged citizenry—one that insists on participation and a voice in its future.

No system can endure without the support—even tacit support—of the people it claims to serve.

The only path back to the American Dream is to resuscitate and restore democracy.

While individual issues matter, the deeper problem is a deficit of democracy. We must shift from an issue-based approach to a systemic one—replacing today's neoliberal system, dominated by a small economic elite, with a humane, sustainable, democratic system.

The only way to succeed is through a broad, visible coalition of citizens rallying under the banner of democracy.

Once we've made that shift, we must build the infrastructure needed to sustain democracy.

144

Back to Basics: Eyes on the Prize

The prize is a return to our democratic heritage—
choosing democracy over elite rule.

The method is to repopulate and restore the core
institutions of democracy.

Stay focused, even under pressure from the powerful
economic elite; don't get distracted by side issues.

As a society, we must recover without vengeance—a test
of character and maturity.

Unity, unity, unity—the elite will use every tactic to divide
and weaken us.

We are facing a wounded, well-armed behemoth willing
to do whatever it takes to regain control.

Rebuilding a sustainable democracy will require
infrastructure dedicated to that purpose.

The ultimate victory: a vibrant, inclusive democracy that
reestablishes the value of citizenship and offers a
platform to solve human problems cooperatively.

Conclusions

An American Earthquake and the Watershed Moment

We must remember that the disorienting election of 2016 was simply one more watershed event similar to the three previous watershed events we survived by choosing democracy overrule by an economic aristocracy. We have been here before, historically, and we found the courage to, not only survive, but to become stronger in the process. This is the challenge for this generation of Americans…a chance to, once again, become a "Greatest Generation" on our own merits.

We have always found ways to unite under the banner of Democracy, to call up the power of the American Spirit within the citizenry and to carry the day.

The elections of 2016 were a political and social earthquake that shattered all the illusions so carefully put into place over several decades by the neoliberal establishment. That establishment had been hard at work undermining our humanity and our democracy and transferring wealth and power to its inner members.

Over the last several decades, in some ways since the death of FDR, an economic aristocracy has been hard at work trying to reassert itself as the dominating influence in this nation. Politics has been one of the tools it has used, and it has used it very effectively.

At first there was rather subtle push-back against New Deal programs and unions, beginning with regulations and controls. Then there was the fear of Communism and the Cold War focusing on conformity, the military, a security system and great expenditures making corporations some of the key elements and therefore making the economic elite central to that process.

Doing whatever was necessary to build these systems began to chip away at the oversight and regulatory systems. Meanwhile capitalism was beginning to be given cover as being integral to democracy, eventually becoming the focus of our foreign policy though under the guise of spreading democracy.

All of this is given an international flavor with such organizations as the World Bank and the IMF (International Monetary Fund), later to be followed by globalization and trade pacts formulated mostly by corporate need and greed.

An entire ideology…neoliberal economics…was born to justify the message and to create and continue the illusion that everyone would benefit from this program.

By now an entire, complex establishment had been formed to sustain and expand the illusion.

Then the system began to falter, the illusion began to be exposed.

For the last several years cracks in that illusion were becoming apparent to more and more people. Everyone began to see who prospered and who was asked to make the sacrifices.

The election of 2016 suddenly offered a voice for change and a return to democratic values with the candidacy of Bernie Sanders. People responded as his message resonated with the realities of the real lives of so many citizens. He was about to be swept into the White House, allowing a real chance for change.

The establishment of the economic elite saw what that would mean for their continuation and did whatever was necessary to neutralize that threat. Eventually they used the establishment elements of the Democratic National Committee to find a way to derail the Sanders' campaign.

147

The problem, however, was that the message of change had been articulated and had energized the populace. Now, left with only two options, neither of which energized them, they either stayed away or voted for a very flawed change agent (better than the same-old, same-old).

So, the power of the economic elite continued in a somewhat different form, but still intact (just see what has happened to the stock market after the election). However, the illusion was pretty well shattered, and a more top-down regime of imposed solutions took its place, with fear and secrecy, distrust, and polarization.

The citizenry were left with clear, but stark, options. They could continue on the same trajectory with their eyes wide open to the consequences; or they could begin the arduous, grass-roots trek away from the flawed economic model and back toward an inclusive and sustainable future with democracy.

Reviewing How We Got Here: An Historical Perspective

Those who wanted an economic elite to rule and those who sided with a democracy of citizens were contending with each other in this nation, from the very beginning. Those who wanted an aristocracy of wealth to rule saw the American Revolution as an opportunity to substitute an American aristocracy of wealth for the English one.

The need to hold out the hope of democracy to enlist the help of the rest of the populace was, perhaps seen as a necessary evil. The idea of democracy was a powerful and intoxicating belief which took hold with the ordinary citizens and could never be totally stifled.

The battle lines were formed, and the decades were filled with continuing skirmishes. Mostly the economic elite won and often dominated the leadership, but there was always the strong undercurrent of democracy that needed to be dealt with to continue in power.

When the dominance of that wealthy elite got too much hubristic power in the 1920s it nearly destroyed the nation.

FDR was elected and the difficult rebuilding of a democratic foundation began in earnest. It was a slow and arduous process supported by a majority of the citizens but bitterly opposed by the economic elite, still sure that their autocratic ideas of rule were a better choice.

It took a war to get the nation back on a relatively sound footing, but after FDR's death the forces of the economic elite began to chip away at the progress of democracy. They were relentless and had the financing to organize ways to get their message out.

They were ultimately successful under the banner of neoliberal economics.

Saving Democracy-2025

How We Extricate Ourselves

To extricate ourselves we need to deal with the frustration of being intentionally misled and bilked of both our resources and our democracy. We need to understand the psychology of victimhood and recovery and not fall into the patterns of vengeance and punishment which will only use the valuable time and energy needed to move forward in a positive way.

If we realize that the alien economic system that now rules us is a divergence from our democratic heritage, we will begin to walk away from it and back toward our more balanced and sustainable democracy again.

This will require courage and risk and will only work if we stay together using the support and energy that our numbers carry with them.

Ultimate Goal: Democracy First

This is a watershed moment for America. Will the American Spirit of our rich heritage come back to life and lead us back to the promised land of democracy or will we simply continued to be guided by this economic elite toward their ultimate domination and our demise as a free people?

It is time to change the narrative back to the democratic narrative and walk away from the thoroughly discredited narrative of neoliberal economics which has led us to the brink of our own destruction and perhaps, the destruction of a planet that can support human life.

As with any crisis, we need to unify to take advantage of the strengths we have. Our major strength is in our overwhelming numbers, but to effectively use that strength, we need to unify and recognize that we can't win the confrontation with countless small and independent armies fighting skirmishes within a battleground chosen by the very enemy we are trying to defeat.

150

Our numbers reflect our inclusiveness, accepting all who believe in democracy enough to stand up and fight for it. If we realize the power of unifying under the banner of democracy, we will enhance all the independent issues that smaller groups have been working on. This unity simply multiplies the effectiveness and makes it clear to anyone-especially politician-who observe what is happening. It is like putting all the puzzle pieces together to form a glorious picture of the power of an inclusive democracy.

This change will also change the focus from a soulless and heartless, engineered, mechanical model of market-based neoliberal economics, with its marketplace morality and it's monetizing of life and ultimately destroying that life and the planet in its pursuit of economic growth. It will be a change back to a humanized and sustainable world.

It will be a reclaiming of this nation once more for the citizens and an end to the alien ideology that has been occupying this nation and that has been destroying democracy and the future of this nation and its people.

It is time to hook our individual and group actions to the Democratic Train leading back to our heritage. It is time to couple our hopes with each other, once again, and to follow our hearts and hopes to a sustainable and inclusive human future.

Remember, we do not need anyone's permission to do what is right and important for our survival. We do not need to wait to pass a law, we can just do what is necessary to make a system that works for the citizens of America.

The final solution is to embrace democracy once again...Democracy today, Democracy for the future and Democracy forever.

If we do not unite under the banner of Democracy now, we will be defeated in a series of large and small battles and skirmishes within the neoliberal economic system, finally losing the war with only massive casualties to show for our struggles.

Get aboard now for hope, for a democracy, for a sustainable future.

Boots on the ground will trump money in the bank if we present a united front.

Viva the Human Spirit and the return of the American Dream!

Democracy First!

Hope Abounds: The Transition is Occurring

The Journey

This is a journey back to democracy that is a grassroots process. Remember that journey means the distance one can travel in a day, so it focuses on the process and not solely on the destination. And remember that the word, destination, is from the same root as destiny…that which is foreordained. Perhaps democracy has been our real manifest destiny all along and the root of the real American Dream energized by the power of the American Spirit.

Out of Our Past

Throughout our history as a nation, during more democratic periods as well as those more autocratic times, there has always been a strong strain of active work toward more democratic reform. Sometimes they toiled in obscurity, sometime within less mainstream movements, and at times within the union movement.

All of these folks kept the flame of possible democratic improvement alive, often on a very lonely grassroots level.

Transition in Process

At this time there are many who are in the process of making the transition back to more democratic practices, some of which they never left.

There are those who practice organic farming and those who actively support healthy foods. There are those who support community banking and community businesses. There are those who work on environmental issues. There are

153

those who work to limit war and violence. There are those who work to rebuild a sense of community and public services.

There are people and groups who give their time and resources to help those who are being left out and provide services for those in need.

There are places that have moved to public funding of elections, New York City for example. There are places that are using ranked-choice voting.

There are also cities, municipalities and communities that are making the transition without waiting for permission from the top.

There are, and have always been, politicians who truly serve the citizens and work tirelessly to be sure those interests continue to be expressed.

Without much effort you can find a myriad of people and groups who are now traveling that road back to democracy.

Our Young Citizens

Lest we forget, young citizens are very active supporting the transition back to a sustainable democratic future.

They have seen how empty and irrelevant the current establishment has become, and they see the destructiveness of neoliberal economics which has spread death and destruction across the globe in search of domination and profit.

They have seen that this narrative has led to unnecessary divisions and rejection of too many people. They cannot understand why we older folk are still willing to support such systems when there are so clearly more positive options available.

Young people are very active in this process. One of the most notable examples has been the youth movement that won a case against the government for not acting as responsible stewards of the environment and threatening their futures. The group is known as Our Children's Trust.

The Creativity of the American Dream

The possibility of returning to the richness of the American Dream once more and the return of hope for a sustainable future releases all kinds of creativity and entrepreneurship for the future.

The Resilient American Spirit

And finally, this newly empowered citizenry will flex its muscles to show the American resilience that democracy releases. Everyone will be willing to roll up their sleeves and get back to work as a society to proudly rebuild an inclusive society we can all treasure.

Reviewing Perspectives

It is worthwhile to remember that we have been living in a kind of American Oz that has been shaken into perspective with the American Earthquake of the election of 2016. That was an opportunity to see what caused the earthquake…the final eruption of the friction caused by the tectonic plate dominated by economics riding up over the more humanized democratic plate until the pressure became too much to restrain.

As we gained clarity, we also saw how well constructed that dominant economic system had constructed an establishment to serve, consolidate, expand, and defend it. We recognized the town, the castle, the temple and the wall and the roles they played in supporting a new world view.

155

It was not unlike an alien invasion, replacing human responses with responses based only on economics.

To make all that change an article of faith, we fell under the spell of a new civic religion, the Church of Wealth with chapels in nearly every town and city.

We watched as the humanness was hollowed out of our societies, our businesses, our government and institutions and our communities. The reigning philosophy of neoliberal economics allowed a disconnect from the realities of nations, of the environment and, ultimately, the planet itself. It allowed the ruling theory to become untethered from the human realities of the planet, operating like some kind of Death Star, disconnected and ready to punish any who did not comply with their wishes.

Eventually that ruling elite became addicted to that wealth and power and is willing to feed that addiction at any price.

In recent years that establishment had started to show cracks and had begun to crumble, requiring more attention to maintenance and harsher measures to force compliance.

The establishment is in its final death throes and has pulled out all the stops. That establishment has many tools at its disposal and now has a new engineer who cares little about what anyone else thinks. He will impose his single-minded vision on the society, come hell or high water.

Saving Democracy-2025

Because it is a watershed moment, we must choose either to continue on with the neoliberal Dystopian Express or choose to transfer to the Democratic Local headed back to a sustainable and balanced democracy.

This is a watershed moment — the "All Aboard" moment.

As the neoliberal economic establishment is shown to be a hollow illusion and a new direction is clearly needed, those caught in the web of deceit and betrayal must kick the spell of dependency and, like recovering from a bad divorce, must understand the psychology of spells, the spell of victimhood and how to spell their way out of it.

Afterward

What People Want

All of this is in the context of what ordinary people are really hoping for in their lives. Although everyone craves some form of recognition and respect from their society and their peers, and although nearly everyone is ambitious to provide a good life for themselves, their loved ones and their society, most people are not expecting to become rich and famous and are totally OK with that. Most people are simply wanting to survive and to have a peaceful life, willingly working hard at some kind of productive work and living with their families in a supportive society that offers a sustainable future for them.

When given the option, they tend to see more to be gained from cooperation and a sense of a supportive community than trying to handle the vicissitudes of life by themselves, with distrust, defensiveness and competition for survival.

There will be some competition within that more inclusive society, but it will be more like the friendly competition of fishing or golf, on the basketball or tennis courts, or the softball diamond. It is not the kind of competition that breeds distance nor a significant sense of winners or losers.

They just want to be able to go on with their lives as a part of a peaceful and humane society.

Saving Democracy-2025

Section II: Since 2016
The Unfolding Crisis

Much has happened since that presidential election of 2016. Let me highlight some of the more significant events.

The First Trump Administration

During the first Trump administration, we watched as an alien ideology took hold—an ideology that sought to dismantle regulation and oversight in the name of unleashing American business. With a sweeping corporate tax cut—from 35% to 21%—wealth continued its migration to the top, deepening income inequality to levels not seen since the Gilded Age and the crash of 1929. Wages stagnated, while the stock market surged.

Trump's attacks on the judiciary and intelligence agencies marked a break from presidential norms. He bypassed Congress with executive orders, pushed anti-immigrant policies including family separations at the Mexican border under a zero-tolerance rule, and implemented a travel ban targeting several Muslim-majority countries. He began construction on sections of a U.S.–Mexico border wall. Perhaps the most lasting legacy of his first term was his appointment of three deeply conservative justices to the U.S. Supreme Court—shifting its ideological balance for a generation.

Internationally, Trump withdrew the United States from the Paris Climate Accord and the Iran Nuclear Deal, and applied pressure on NATO allies to increase their financial contributions. He launched a trade war with China, renegotiated NAFTA into the USMCA, and famously met with Kim Jong-un—with few tangible results.

Then came the global COVID-19 pandemic. The economy ground to a halt. There was urgent need for federal leadership—support for scientific research, vaccine development, and public health infrastructure. Trump's response to the pandemic was widely criticized. Many health experts argued that his downplaying of the crisis, mocking of mask-wearing, and promotion of misinformation contributed to public confusion and may have worsened outcomes.

The nation began to fracture. The rift between truth and conspiracy widened. "Fake news" became a battle cry. Science was mocked. Global warming dismissed. Public discourse collapsed into ideological warfare. Trump cast himself as a law-and-order strongman against such protests as Black Lives Matter, particularly after the killing of George Floyd in Minneapolis. He embraced extremism and turned political division into political fuel.

There were two attempts to impeach Donald Trump—in 2019 and again in 2021. Both failed. The Republican Party stood firmly behind him, regardless of the charges or evidence presented.

The Democratic Party

Meanwhile, the Democratic Party spent much of its time spinning Hillary Clinton's 2016 loss: blaming Russian interference, blaming whistleblowers who exposed her private emails and the DNC's sabotage of Bernie Sanders, blaming latent sexism, or blaming Sanders supporters themselves. But rarely did the Party look inward. Rarely did it question its own leadership, its strategies, or its political blindness that had caused it to miss a tectonic shift happening beneath its feet, the rise of ordinary Americans, long ignored, now becoming a powerful and disillusioned force.

The old politics had died. And with it, the familiar outlines of both political parties. The Republican Party had become the vehicle of Trump's personal movement. The Democratic Party, in its corporate coziness and centrism, had become something like a lighter version of the old GOP. It was time to admit that the political terrain had changed—and so had the rules.

The 2020 Election and the Insurrection

When 2020 came, the Democrats stumbled into the presidential campaign like a scene from Dumb and Dumber. With 29 candidates initially, and about 20 still in the race at one point, they seemed to believe that replicating the Republican circus of 2016 would somehow produce a winning formula. It was a disheartening spectacle. And in the end, they chose a cautious, middle-of-the-road figure in Joe Biden—a man firmly tied to the lineage of Clinton, Obama, and the politics of the past.

Biden won, but just barely—and largely because a significant number of Americans were voting against Trump, not necessarily for Biden. But Trump wasn't finished. He cast himself as the ultimate political victim. He claimed the election was fraudulent, that it had been stolen. He called his followers to Washington on January 6, 2021.

That day, the world watched as a mob stormed the Capitol, seeking to stop the certification of the election. The House Chambers were breached, and members of Congress were forced to flee or hide. It was an insurrection—an attack on democracy itself—unlike anything the nation had ever witnessed. The social fissures that had long been forming now cracked wide open. What had once seemed like political polarization had become a dangerous, and possibly permanent, fracture in American unity.

The Biden Years

The Biden years were marked by charge and counForcharge, trial delays, legal maneuvering, and ongoing fallout from the Trump presidency. Trump faced multiple indictments—some for election interference, others for obstruction or fraud. While legal proceedings dragged on, a congressional committee investigated the January 6th insurrection, producing volumes of evidence, witness testimony, and findings. Hundreds of insurrectionists were prosecuted and imprisoned. Yet the national unrest remained—and in many ways, deepened.

Still, government returned to more familiar rhythms. The U.S. rejoined the Paris Climate Accord and the World Health Organization. Biden worked to restore America's international standing, reassuring allies and reaffirming commitments to NATO. On the domestic front, his administration responded to the ongoing COVID-19 pandemic—distributing vaccines, funding relief efforts, and trying to stabilize a battered economy.

But this was not the same America Biden had once served as Vice President. The nation had changed. Mistrust ran deep. Any federal intervention—even public health measures—was viewed with suspicion by large segments of the population. Mask mandates, vaccines, even basic scientific guidance became culture-war flashpoints. The divide between civic duty and personal liberty had grown into a chasm.

For many, the final takeaway seemed to be that economic continuity should have taken precedence, and government interference was viewed as unnecessary overreach.

Still, Biden pushed forward. He passed an infrastructure bill. He took steps to fight inflation. He supported labor unions, pushed to raise the minimum wage, and sought relief for student loan debt holders. He stood up for reproductive rights after the Supreme Court overturned Roe v. Wade, and worked to protect LGBTQ+ rights, civil rights, and voting access—all while facing a hostile Supreme Court and a divided Congress.

Internationally, Biden managed the final U.S. withdrawal from Afghanistan—ending a 20-year war that had cost thousands of lives and trillions of dollars. It was a necessary but chaotic exit that exposed deep dysfunction in American foreign policy.

Biden also responded forcefully to Russia's invasion of Ukraine, offering strong U.S. support and encouraging European NATO support. But to some, this marked a return to Cold War-era proxy politics. Ukraine became the buffer state between NATO and Russia, just as South and Central America had once served as a buffer for the U.S. against socialism in the Western Hemisphere. The echoes of U.S. policy in Cuba, Chile, Nicaragua, and elsewhere could still be heard—and still shaped our instincts.

Gaza

When Israeli Prime Minister Benjamin Netanyahu launched a massive military assault on Gaza, the Biden administration offered unwavering support. For many Americans—and much of the world—it was a moment of moral reckoning. The scale of destruction, the deliberate targeting of civilian infrastructure, and the blockade of food and medical aid painted a picture not of defense, but of collective punishment. The word "genocide" began appearing not just in international press, but in statements from global leaders and human rights organizations.

The United States not only backed Israel diplomatically—it armed it, shielded it from UN censure, and silenced dissent at home. Public demonstrations in support of Palestine were met with fierce institutional resistance. Pro-Palestinian voices were vilified. Even speaking on behalf of the Palestinian people was increasingly labeled antisemitic-a term weaponized to shut down discussion rather than combat actual hate.

The U.S. withdrew its support from the UN Relief and Works Agency (UNRWA), choking off a critical lifeline for millions of displaced and starving Palestinians. In the face of these actions, a growing number of Americans—particularly young people and minority communities—faced a moral crisis. Many found themselves unable to support a political party that had enabled this level of brutality-without debate, without transparency, and seemingly without conscience.

The 2024 Election

When Kamala Harris became the Democratic nominee in 2024—replacing Biden, who chose not to run again—she refused to allow the U.S. policy on Gaza to be questioned. That decision alone may have cost the Democrats the election. A vital segment of the progressive and youth vote simply could not be rallied.

The 2024 election was shaped by chaos, legal ambiguity, and political trauma. Trump's legal problems were front and center—but his future, ironically, depended on his ability to return to the presidency. The nation remained deeply polarized. The aftermath of the January 6 insurrection was still being adjudicated. The Republican narrative of "rigged elections," "fake news," and a deep-state witch hunt persisted—now even more entrenched.

Trump's campaign was bombastic and unrelenting. He promised retribution, vengeance, and national purification. His base cheered. Immigration was again his main weapon, stoking fear and resentment. Inflation and the cost of living provided the emotional fuel. And the Democrats, still not really acknowledging the change in the political realities of the nation, could not mount a compelling counter-narrative that effectively spoke to the unhappiness of the ordinary American voter.

And, as had become increasingly true, the campaigns of both parties were funded with dark money; the Republican side especially by some of the richest billionaires in the world.

So, the people voted. Trump won. Kamala Harris conceded. There was a peaceful transition of power-as democracy required.

But what followed was anything but peaceful.

The First 100 Days: The Second Trump Administration

Some might call what occurred after Donald Trump's second inauguration "Armageddon."

After his inauguration, the transformation was swift. The Great Purge was on.

Trump began ruling by executive fiat, issuing nearly 150 executive orders within his first 100 days. One of his first moves was to pardon and stop the trials of those who had participated in the January 6th Insurrection. That should have told us all we needed to know about his vision.

He also fired key legal officials, like Inspector Generals and senior military leaders who were perceived as disloyal. He moved quickly to dismantle large swaths of the federal government, starting with the Department of Education and public health services.

165

With Elon Musk installed as head of a new administrative apparatus called DOGE (Department of Government Efficiency), the slashing of the federal bureaucracy began in earnest. Veterans Affairs, Medicare, public health programs, and even weather and disaster response systems were gutted. Massive layoffs followed. Expertise was devalued. Loyalty to Trump appeared to become the sole job qualification.

Trump's cabinet was filled with inexperienced but camera-friendly appointees who pledged personal loyalty over institutional competence. The Department of Justice was hollowed out and reshaped to serve his interests—legally, politically, personally.

Immigration policy became brutal. Due process was ignored. Entire communities were targeted. Deportations increased sharply, including mass roundups of immigrants—some with legal status, others without. People—including citizens—were being arrested off the street, sometimes by unidentified masked men in unmarked vehicles, often without legal explanation. This began to include judges and even mayors. Some were sent to ICE detention centers, some to offshore prisons in El Salvador. Legal counsel and judicial review became afterthoughts.

And it didn't stop there.

Foreign students—even those with valid legal status—who had participated in pro-Palestinian protests or written sympathetic letters and op-eds, were detained.

They were sent to detention facilities, sometimes far from home, under the vague auspices of national security. Civil liberties were treated as obstacles. Dissent was redefined as disloyalty.

What was happening was not just political overreach—it was a full-blown restructuring of American governance. The blitzkrieg of executive orders and bureaucratic purges was

Saving Democracy-2025

anything but random. It was strategic. It followed the blueprint of Project 2025. It seemed like something that Naomi Klein had described in her book, *The Shock Doctrine*: first you create great trauma to the system and while people are overwhelmed by trauma, a new system can be slipped in under cover of confusion.

This was the American version of shock and awe. While citizens were stunned by the speed and severity of the changes, a new regime quietly installing itself—seemingly hostile to democratic traditions and indifferent to constitutional limits. The government was being weaponized against American citizens, the rule of law was being challenged, due process ignored and the Constitution itself seemingly at risk.

Congress appeared mesmerized. The courts, weakened and outmaneuvered, attempted delaying actions. Institutional checks and balances buckled under the weight of authoritarian speed and audacity.

Section III-
Understanding the Quiet
Manipulation of the
Economic Elite

From the 2016 Political Earthquake to our 2025 Watershed Moment

The disorienting 2016 election was not an anomaly. It could have been a watershed moment—like others in our history—when the nation was called to choose between democracy and rule by an economic aristocracy. But neither the nation nor the political parties were ready to make that decision. That watershed moment is now, in 2025, and a decision is urgently needed.

We've been here before. And each time, we've found the courage not just to survive, but to grow stronger. This is the challenge of our generation—a chance to become a "Greatest Generation" in our own right.

We've always been able to rally under the banner of democracy, to summon the American spirit from within the citizenry and carry the day. But 2016 was different. It was a political and social earthquake that shattered decades of illusion—illusions carefully constructed by a neoliberal establishment more interested in serving the economic elite than the common good.

Reviewing American History

To understand this struggle, two images are helpful.

168

The first is the image of our history as following two sets of railway tracks, laid side by side from the beginning, each moving toward an American future. One set of tracks led toward democracy—toward shared prosperity and civic participation. The other, more discreet but equally powerful, led toward private wealth and corporate control. For a time, the two sets of tracks seemed parallel, perhaps even compatible. But history shows us what happens when they diverge.

The second image is of two tectonic plates forming the history of American politics, seen as a vast landscape shaped by those two great tectonic plates. One plate represents the ordinary citizen and the ideal of democracy; the other represents the economic elite and the accumulation of capital and power. For long periods, these plates moved uneasily but without catastrophic upheaval. But when the tension between them became too great, they produced political earthquakes that reshaped the terrain.

One such rupture came with the Civil War—when the contradiction of slavery in a democracy shattered the illusion of unity and revealed the irreconcilable tension between democracy and domination. Though slavery ended, the assassination of Lincoln allowed the economic elite to hijack Reconstruction and reassert control.

Another rupture came in 1929, when unrestrained capitalism triggered the Great Depression. Out of that crisis came the rise of the voices of the ordinary people. The result being FDR and the New Deal, a moment when the government operated in service to the people. The train of democracy was momentarily back on track and dominant.

But the elite never accepted that loss of control. With FDR's death, their long campaign to reclaim dominance resumed. Anti-communism became their tool. The Cold War narrative cast capitalism as synonymous with democracy, and Russia—our former ally—as the ultimate threat. That conflict was, at heart, the conflict of capitalism and its nemesis, communism.

That reframing allowed the economic elite to rebuild power under cover of patriotism. Military spending soared. The CIA expanded. And the voices of ordinary people were again pushed aside.

The Threat of John F. Kennedy

As the McCarthy era began to fade, a hunger grew among ordinary Americans for something more stable, more humane. John F. Kennedy offered that possibility—a return to idealism, to shared progress, to a future in which everyday citizens mattered.

But Kennedy's vision—like Lincoln's before him—threatened the dominance of the economic elite. And so, another political rupture followed. The assassinations of JFK, Martin Luther King Jr., and Robert Kennedy removed the leading voices of a newly awakening democratizing movement. The result was turbulence—culminating in the chaos of the 1968 Democratic Convention in Chicago. The political system's response was swift: law and order, repression, and the election of Richard Nixon, who promised control over chaos.

Hijacking the Compass and Rerouting the Nation

It was then that those railway tracks began to diverge more sharply.

The democratic track, and its reliable engine, the Democratic Local—focused on equality, shared prosperity, and civic participation—began to be ignored. The track of the economic elite, now fully empowered, began to curve hard to the right and began laying new tracks toward an economic future, tracks for the Dystopian Express. A new narrative emerged, selling the promise of freedom as personal financial success, and promoting capitalism not just as an economic system, but as the highest expression of human development.

The compass was redirected: the true north of democracy replaced by a new one—capitalism and neoliberal economics, and the magnetism of wealth seemed to be overwhelming.

This shift was formalized in 1971 with the Powell Memorandum, a strategic blueprint encouraging corporate America to engage aggressively in politics and to finally dominate politics and the direction of the nation.

What followed was the neoliberal age: deregulation, privatization, trickle-down economics, the expansion of corporate lobbying, and the emergence of a powerful financial sector that made money from money—detached from the productive labor of citizens. Government began to serve markets, not people.

The train that once promised to carry Americans toward a more inclusive future was now replaced by what we might call the Dystopian Express. No longer a single unified train for a common destination, the system split into a stratified train:

At the front: The luxury cars of the economic elite, gliding smoothly toward financial nirvana-detached from the rest of the train.

Immediately behind them: The aspiring elite, consultants and influencers, living in comfort while clearing the path ahead and shielding those in front.

Farther back: The working classes—white-collar and blue-collar—still laboring under the illusion that hard work alone would move them forward.

Toward the end: The marginalized—immigrants, the poor, racial and religious minorities—crammed into

171

overcrowded, unsanitary cars, seen as expendable labor or social ballast.

Trailing the whole procession: The prison cars. The law enforcement trains. The surveillance cars. Built not to serve but to control.

As this Dystopian Express moved ever onward, the remnants of a tattered democracy were left behind.

The longer this system ran, the more distorted the distribution of benefits became. Wealth and political voice were concentrated in the front cars. Meanwhile, those in the back—who powered the entire system—were forgotten. Anger simmered. Pressure built. The tectonic plates began to shift again.

The people in the rear began to look for someone who valued them—someone who heard them, who would validate their frustration. In the 2016 campaign, Bernie Sanders gave voice to that longing. Bernie spoke of fairness, of justice, of rebalancing society and reclaiming the democratic route. But the Democratic Party—now itself riding comfortably in the upper cars—silenced his message. The DNC blocked his rise, extinguishing the one mainstream leader who might have shifted the ordinary citizens back to the old set of tracks leading to a democratic future for all citizens.

Without a real progressive populist, concerned with the welfare of the ordinary citizen, that unclaimed political constituency turned toward another leader and another message. A message focused on victimhood, unfairness, frustration and anger. He played to their biases and gave them enemies, demonizing immigrants, foreign ideas, liberals, fake news, and untrustworthy science, medicine, or explanations built on a now rejected logic.

So, this underrepresented constituency turned to a demagogic pseudo-populist salesman: Donald Trump.

Donald Trump was no man of the people—he came from wealth and power. But he spoke their anger. He named their enemies. He gave them not democracy, but an outlet to their frustration. He promised action and perhaps even vengeance.

The result was the earthquake of the 2016 election—a jolt that shattered illusions and exposed the new topography of American politics. The tectonic rupture was complete. The tracks toward a democratic future had been abandoned. The new train, The Dystopian Express was now headed somewhere very different—and very dangerous.

Where We Are Now

Since that seismic disruption in 2016, the political landscape has shifted. One party, now firmly the party of Donald Trump, understands that change and has found ways to exploit that change to their advantage by focusing the frustration and anger of that newly immerged political constituency to threaten, and perhaps, even destroy the status quo. The nation has become polarized. Meanwhile, the Dystopian Express continues its rush to its destination, full control of the nation by an economic elite, finalizing what might be seen as a quiet coup, having begun in the 1960s.

With Donald Trump as the engineer of that Dystopian Express, it appears that he has little interest in preserving democracy. One might think that his goal is to transform the nation into "USA, Incorporated", seeing himself not so much as president, but as a CEO. The structure might resemble a corporate model, with cabinet secretaries acting as divisional leaders in this new dominant corporation, following the vision of the CEO and answerable to him alone. If there were to be a Board of Directors, it would be his billionaire friends. The ultimate goal of such an enterprise could well be not only to produce profit, but to also control and manipulate the markets and the ordinary citizens, in such a way as to make them dependable and predictable. In such a case, the nation could now be used as a veritable "weapon of mass destruction" to overcome any obstacles.

This represents the final betrayal—not just of our institutions, but of the people whose pain and energy made this political shift possible. The very citizens who deserved to be heard have instead been weaponized, then discarded.

They were once the base of democracy. And now, once again, they are being left behind.

174

And so, the great American train, once bound for a democratic future, has been hijacked. The new route—laid by and for the economic elite—leaves behind the towns, the workers, the citizens who built the tracks.

The earthquake of 2016 was not just the beginning. It revealed how far we had already drifted from our democratic path. What we face now is not merely a political challenge—it is an ethical and a moral one.

Will we continue riding the Dystopian Express, content to serve a corporate empire that no longer even pretends to serve us? Or will we reclaim our democratic destiny, reboard the dependable "Democratic Local," and restore the vision of a nation built by—and for—its people?

The choice remains ours. But time is running short.

Section IV-
Awakening the Citizens

A Call to Action

And yet—not all is lost.

In the final measure, the only force capable of stopping this demolition of democracy is the action of a unified citizenry itself.

That is the challenge of democracy: not merely to be governed, but to govern. To participate. To insist that our voices matter, and to demand that power be exercised in service to the people—not against them. In this moment, citizenship is no longer a passive status. It is a responsibility. If the people fail to act, they will cease to be citizens. They will become subjects, and the American experiment—hard-won, imperfect, and unfinished—may quietly come to an end.

This is a call to action for every citizen who values the right to be heard. The time to act is now, before the destruction becomes irreversible. Destruction happens quickly. It's always easier to burn down than to build up. Rebuilding takes time and careful attention.

We must acknowledge that damage has already been done—damage that will take time and effort to repair. But first, the destruction must be stopped before our democracy is damaged beyond repair, before we are faced with a fait accompli.

The Fate Accompli

Much of it has already become a fait accompli, as illustrated in the story of a well-connected developer who decides to convert a community park into a shopping complex. The park—a cherished space filled with trails, trees, ponds, and a creek—has served generations. It is a place of gathering, reflection, and belonging.

Then one morning, the townspeople wake to the sound of chainsaws. The trees are falling. They rush out to protest, only to be told to take it up with those in charge. When they finally reach the authorities, they're told to get a lawyer. By the time the case is filed, the court date set, and a judgment rendered—weeks later—the park has been clear-cut. Construction has already begun.

Though the court rules the development illegal, the damage is done. The developer offers a perfunctory concession: a token playground and some benches by the new storefronts.

This is what is now happening to the foundational structures of American democracy. The bulldozers have already arrived. We are left with debris, denial, and the slow dawning of a new and dangerous reality.

There is rising concern that Elon Musk and his DOGE team could gain access to sensitive government databases, creating questions of legality, accountability and vulnerability.

We haven't even mentioned the climate crisis—an existential threat not just to democracy, but to human life itself and the entire planet. And yet, the Trump administration has

Saving Democracy-2025

chosen to ignore, deny, and even accelerate the crisis: gutting environmental protections, doubling down on fossil fuel production, and removing all regulatory brakes on carbon emissions.

You might find yourself asking, "How did our leadership allow this?"

But this is not the time to try to find fault or assign blame.

Right now, this emergency demands our full attention and our collective will. If we are to stop the destruction and rebuild the American way of life—our democracy, our communities, our shared future—we must focus. Now.

The traditional American Dream of democracy, inclusivity and justice of compassion and humanitarianism is not the dream of Donald Trump. It is not the dream of Elon Musk. Some might say that Donald Trump is behaving like a delusional autocrat, thumbing his nose at every social, legal, and political norm. And he now seems to control a great number of the levers of government power. It is frightening to consider it is his finger on the nuclear button.

At this point, the legacy of the New Deal is being systematically dismantled. The economic elite have reshaped the United States into a corporate state, what might be seen as "USA Incorporated", where profit is the highest principle—and the presidency, its ultimate executive office; with the President is now CEO-in-Chief, with a duty not to the people, but to extract profits for himself and for his investors, the billionaire class. Departments are streamlined to serve corporate needs. Workers serve at the pleasure of the CEO, department heads and the bottom line.

This is not just a constitutional crisis. It is a moral crisis. And it is a moment of reckoning and there is not a moment to lose. We are now at the final American watershed moment.

Saving Democracy-2025

Citizen Action

Bold and immediate citizen action is all that stands between America remaining a democracy—or collapsing fully into the orbit of something like "USA Incorporated". Ordinary people, standing together, refusing to comply with imposed authoritarian changes, and insisting on their right to shape their own future.

Even in a corporate model, no system can function without its people: no corporation survives without customers, workers, or resources. A democracy is no different. It cannot function without its citizens' support—and cannot be stolen without their silence.

We now stand at another watershed moment. The question before us is stark: Will we reaffirm our commitment to democracy, as generations before us have done; or will we surrender—finally and fatally—to be ruled by an economic elite, accountable to no one else?

We may be nearing a Second American Revolution. But this time, the threat isn't from a foreign empire—or even foreign terrorists. It is a domestic one—a group of oligarchs, billionaires, and ideologues who are may be finishing what they began in the 1960s: a silent, strategic coup, to place the entire government under corporate control. They aim to dismantle the 'American Way of Life'—which is, at its core, democracy.

In the first American Revolution, we faced the most powerful military and naval empire of the time. Now we face a political leader who controls nearly all the levers of domestic power—and is turning those powers against the people themselves. It is daunting, yes. But this fight is no less essential than that first revolution. It may demand our time, our labor, our voices, and even our sacrifice—but it is a fight for the very soul of our democracy. Ours is a democracy that once freed us from tyranny and gave birth to a bold experiment in self-rule. That experiment of democracy and human worth lit a beacon seen around the world. And now the world is watching again. If we fail to keep the ideals of democracy alive here, it will be a blow to the idea of democracy and individual worth around the world.

It may be time for a new generation of citizen soldiers. A new movement of ordinary heroes. Our own Greatest Generation, called not to fight abroad, but to resist a domestic enemy. We will discover the real leaders by seeing who is in the streets with us, not hiding behind desks.

Those in the Trump administration seem to be willing to disregard their oaths of office: an oath to support the Constitution. They've weaponized government against its own people. This is not politics as usual—it is betrayal at the highest order. And it cannot stand.

But the road ahead will not be easy. Nor will it be short. We must steel ourselves for the long haul. We must recommit to the values that founded this nation—not the myths, but the ideals. Not the slogans, but the substance.

Democracy has never been guaranteed. It must be renewed. Defended. Reclaimed. Again, and again.

Let us begin with clarity and resolve. Let's look at what must be done—and how to begin.

Methods: Tools, Techniques and Tactics

1: Reclaiming Democracy—A Citizen's Mission

The American Dream has been captured by elite interests. This is no longer a hypothetical threat—it is our current reality. Yet history shows that when democracy has been most at risk, citizens have found ways to reclaim it.

Our mission today is to renew democracy through grassroots power, shared vision, and active participation. The goal is not just resistance—it is renewal, reconstruction, and reconnection to our democratic roots.

2: Foundations for Action

Democracy begins with principle: shared power, participation, justice, and compassion.

This movement doesn't require permission. It welcomes all who value inclusive democracy and are willing to help build it—together.

- **The Spirit Required**

Courage and persistence
Faith in the human spirit
Creativity and cooperation
Resilience and belief in democracy's necessity

3: Tools

This toolkit offers practical, creative, and structural tactics any citizen or community can use to strengthen democracy from the ground up.

- **Practical Tools**

Organize community circles and public forums

Write letters, make calls, and engage public officials

Launch alternative media channels and local newsletters

Host teach-ins, rallies, and public events

Use social media to share democratic stories and calls to action

Build intergenerational communities-we are all in this together

Hold members of Congress accountable—remind them they serve constituents, not just donors

Creative Action

Use art, music, and poetry to express democratic values

Stage public performances and street demonstrations

Employ powerful metaphors (e.g., The Dystopian Express vs. The Democratic Local)

Infrastructure Building

Create a digital clearinghouse of ideas, actions, and resources

Launch participatory budgeting and citizen decision-making efforts

Reinvest in public institutions like libraries, public schools, and healthcare

4: Strategic Projects for Democratic Renewal

These initiatives build on the Citizen Toolkit by offering larger collective campaigns that can help reshape culture, reclaim public institutions, and renew our democratic spirit. Each project offers a pathway toward tangible impact—connecting personal action to systemic change.

- **1. Democracy First: Anchor every initiative in democratic principle.**

Before we can solve issues of economics, policy, or governance, we must restore democratic structures that ensure fair participation and accountability. Without functioning democratic institutions, our concerns cannot be openly discussed or effectively resolved.

- **2. Board the Democracy Local: Reframe action as choosing a new track.**

This metaphor invites people to imagine themselves boarding a different kind of political train: one where democracy is the destination, and economic concerns are managed as part of—not in place of—that journey. The "Democratic Local" grows in strength by adding "cars" of supporters, movements, and communities committed to justice and inclusion. It is a big umbrella structure.

- **3. Demonstrate for Democracy: Celebrate democracy with peaceful power.**

This project encourages people to live out democratic values in their daily lives—through dialogue, participation, protest, and celebration. Democracy is not only a system; it's a way of being.

- **4. Democracy Register: Track growing support for people-led governance.**

We build an online clearinghouse—a real-time database— to document, connect, and amplify the growing number of people, groups, and communities aligning with democratic renewal.

- **5. Take Back the Establishment: Reclaim public institutions for the public good.**

This initiative encourages citizens to attend civic meetings, school boards, and public forums—and to speak up as representatives of everyday people. The goal is to ensure that the voice of the citizen is once again present in the rooms where decisions are made.

- **6. Project to Save Democracy (PTSD): Healing the democratic spirit.**

Our democracy has been traumatized. This project is about civic healing: restoring faith in democratic process, reconnecting people to shared purpose, and rebuilding emotional and spiritual resilience.

Section 5: Movement Sustainability

Sustainable change requires more than passion—it demands structure, discipline, and personal renewal. Democracy is not a one-time event; it is a living culture, a shared system, and a long-term commitment.

If democracy is to survive and flourish, citizens must not only act—but also endure. That means staying engaged even when the path is hard, and the results are slow. It also means finding and maintaining your political voice—as individuals and communities.

- **Reclaiming and Sustaining Our Voice**

Finding your political voice begins with knowing that you have one. Speak at town halls. Write op-eds. Mentor new activists. Share your values in conversations, classrooms, and campaigns. Help others discover their voices too—especially those who've been ignored, discouraged, or left out.

Democracy flourishes when its people speak up and stand together.

- **Sustaining Elements**

Build a political party that truly represents ordinary citizens. At present, neither major party seems fully willing to embrace this mission.

Enact fair laws and support strong, independent institutions

Keep educating and adapting—democracy must evolve to survive

Celebrate progress—small and large—to renew morale

Stay vigilant—forces of elite control will always seek to reassert themselves

Encourage reflection and rest—democracy requires resilience

Section 6: Final Call to Action

Democracy is not something we inherit—it is something we create, again and again.

This is our watershed moment. The choice is ours.

Let's choose democracy. Let's build it. Together.

Perspective: The Music of Democracy

Voices rule the world. There are the solo voices of monarchs, dictators, military leaders, and strongmen of the world whose voices soar loud and strong above the, sometimes angry, hive-like, humming of their citizens.

Then there are the larger singing groups—oligarchs, ruling elites, aristocracies, and religious authorities—who claim to sing the nation's song, but do so only in unison, allowing no harmony from other perspectives. It may sound stronger and richer than the solo voices, but it is only unison and still we hear the humming of the voiceless citizens in the background.

And then there was a new sound added. That sound was harmony. As the voices of other segments of the society were added, something magical happened. The music came to life with a new beauty and was heard differently by the citizens. But still there was the hum of those not included and that continued as a distraction.

And then came a new musical idea—Democracy. This new idea planned to include yet more voices. The idea was tried in America, and the new and inspiring sound came from its shores and captivated whole new audiences world-wide. There was actually a certain kind of sacredness in its music that affected people deeply.

Other nations began to try such music, some succeeded, and some were quashed by those who insisted

Saving Democracy-2025

that only solo, or unison music was appropriate for a nation.

In America the chorus grew as new voices were added, always being amazed at the magical transformation of each new voice. There were those, even in America, who thought it was important to limit the number of voices or that there were already too many, liking the earlier harmonies with fewer, selective voices. Some wanted to allow only marshal voices, or the voices of business and commerce, or only religious voices.

Others said that inclusion in the human chorus transformed the ordinariness of their lives into something of gem-like beauty, at times creating incredibly beautiful and unthought of patterns of perfection.

There was dissonance at times, which was fine and expected as long as it did not get to be the focus of the music. With time, it was included, often adding unexpected new richness and dimension to the compositions.

But the hearts of the people of the world were already enchanted and enamored of the music being created as voices were added. It had become more sacred to them and had touched and enlivened the deepest parts of their humanity. It lifted the human spirit to new heights.

Appendix

A Citizen Toolkit for Action

1. Organize and Mobilize

- Start a local democracy circle or discussion group (e.g., Great Decisions-style).
- Host community meetings to share ideas and build local momentum.
- Create or join issue-focused citizen groups with a democratic foundation.
- Organize local, regional, and national gatherings for pro-democracy causes.
- Form demonstration teams to create peaceful, visible expressions of democratic values.

2. Participate in Democratic Processes

- Register and vote in every election—local, state, and national.
- Encourage universal voting in your community.
- Hold elected officials accountable through coordinated letter-writing, phone calls, emails, and social media campaigns.
- Attend town halls and public hearings to advocate for democratic priorities.
- Track your representatives' voting records and public stances.
- Begin to create a base for a political party that represents the voice and interests of the

188

ordinary citizen. Right now, neither party is willing to wholeheartedly fill that role.

3. Communicate and Educate

- Develop independent media (blogs, podcasts, newsletters) to bypass elite-controlled messaging.
- Create or support alternative news sources rooted in democratic values.
- Use social media strategically to amplify positive democratic messages.
- Tell your story—write op-eds, share personal testimonials, make short videos.
- Counter misinformation with facts, empathy, and clarity.

4. Use Creative Expression as Activism

- Create art, music, or performance pieces that celebrate democracy and civic values.
- Host public exhibits or events that tell the story of American democratic ideals.
- Use storytelling and metaphor to make complex ideas accessible.

5. Build Infrastructure for a Democratic Future

- Establish a clearinghouse of ideas, resources, and networks.
- Reclaim and support public institutions (schools, libraries, postal service, public health).
- Rebuild public trust by demonstrating democratic values in action.

- Support initiatives to reverse privatization of essential public services.
- Develop alternatives to private financial control (e.g., community banks, public credit unions).

6. Cultivate the Democratic Mindset

- Empower others through education and inclusion.
- Celebrate civic participation and small victories publicly.
- Resist bullying, intimidation, and co-optation (especially through seductive funding).
- Promote resilience, hope, and belief in the human spirit.
- Practice non-confrontational activism that emphasizes effective alternatives and peaceful transformation over conflict.

7. Reframe the Narrative

- Challenge the myth of capitalism as democracy—share alternative frameworks.
- Shift focus from profit to people—in conversations, media, and local initiatives.
- Remind others that democracy is a moral choice, not just a political one.
- Adopt and spread the language of the "Democratic Local"—inclusive, collaborative, forward-looking.

8. Finally, Even Small Things Matter.

- Wear a button simply saying "Democracy" or buy a batch to hand out to friends.
- Wear a blue piece of ribbon or even yarn to signify your support of democracy
- Call friends and others to encourage and invite them in
- Remember we are building a "coalition of the willing" by being welcoming and helpful. It is not a time for argument or attempts to change the minds of the "hard core".
- Remember that self-maintenance is important to prevent burn-out, take time for rejuvenation and inspiration.
- Take a break from the mass media and turn off your screens often.
- Fill your life with friends and new acquaintances, music, art, nature, fun and celebration.
- Remember that democracy is intergenerational, requiring the active participation of all citizens, regardless of age or circumstance.

Acknowledgments

No book is ever written in a vacuum, and this one is no exception. *Saving Democracy: From the Warnings of 2016 to the Urgency of 2025* has its roots in a lifetime of experiences, conversations, and relationships—and I am deeply grateful to the many people who have helped shape it.

First and foremost, my deepest thanks go to my wife, **Beth**, my partner of over sixty years. Her unwavering support, thoughtful insights, and steady editorial hand have been essential throughout this journey. She has been both my closest companion and my most trusted reader.

I'm grateful as well to **Tom Hanson**, former foreign service officer and global educator, whose wide-ranging conversations and steady friendship have nourished my thinking and helped refine the ideas in this book.

A heartfelt thanks also goes to the late **Congressman Rick Nolan**, whose wisdom, encouragement, and deep democratic values were an inspiration.

In terms of practical support, I appreciate the guidance of **Beth Kallman Werner** of The Author Connection, and the design skill of **Ben (Ayoub Ben ebri) of** Fiverr, who crafted the cover with care and clarity.

Beyond specific individuals, this book is the product of a life spent learning—from Great Decisions discussion groups, individual empowerment clients, adult education workshops, former students (and even inmates), and fellow citizens engaged in public dialogue. I am also thankful to readers of the original *Saving Democracy*, and to those who have followed and responded to my writing on platforms like LinkedIn, Facebook, Medium, Substack, and OpEdNews.

At the heart of it all is a deep belief in democracy and in the extraordinary potential of ordinary people. I've long been guided by curiosity—about how societies work, how people grow, and how stories, metaphors, and shared meaning help us navigate our world. I believe in the power of context, the importance of perspective, and the capacity of dialogue to spark renewal.

Above all, I am profoundly grateful—for the life I've lived, the support I've received, and the opportunity to reflect and contribute. I have been blessed.

For more on my background and the path that led to this work, see the brief biography that follows.

About the Author

Bob Passi is a lifelong educator, writer, and civic engagement advocate whose career spans public service, teaching, adult education, personal coaching, and community organizing. His work reflects a consistent commitment to personal empowerment, democratic values, and social responsibility.

After growing up in Minnesota, he began his career working in construction and retail while earning his degree from the University of Minnesota—an academic journey that began in engineering and ended in English, enriched by a formative impromptu journey through Europe with a friend. He later worked as an epidemiologist for the U.S. Department of Health, Education and Welfare in New York City, interviewing clients and doing the field work of getting people in for treatment.

Bob went on to teach high school English and American studies in Carson City, Michigan, where his students became some of his most important teachers. Graduate studies at

Michigan State and later the University of Minnesota led to opportunities in curriculum development, adult education, and teaching at the undergraduate level.

He organized international career development conferences, led empowerment workshops, coached individuals in transition, and coordinated public forums including a regional Common Cause conference. Throughout, he remained a passionate advocate for civic engagement and democratic renewal.

Bob's writing blends history, political insight, and personal reflection to explore how systems evolve—and how citizens can reclaim their role in shaping a more just and democratic future.

Email: bobpassi@charter.net
Website: www.perspectives-bobpassi.org